MW01242246

Key Documents in American History
Volume II: 1870 - Present

by Jonathan D. Kantrowitz, Tracey Vasil Biscontini
and Mark Dziak

Edited by Sarah M. Williams

Class Pack ISBN: 978-0-7827-1405-0 • Student Book ISBN: 978-0-7827-1404-3 • © 2006 Queue, Inc.

Queue, Inc. • 80 Hathaway Drive • Stratford, CT 06615
(800) 232-2224 • Fax: (800) 775-2729 • www.qworkbooks.com

Table of Contents

TO THE STUDENTS

In this workbook, you will read many primary source documents about various topics in our nation's history. You will then answer multiple-choice and open-ended questions about what you have read.

As you read and answer the questions, please remember:

- You may refer back to the text as often as you like.

- Read each question very carefully and choose the **best** answer.

- Indicate the correct multiple-choice answers directly in this workbook. Circle or underline the correct answer.

- Write your open-ended responses directly on the lines provided. If you need more space, use a separate piece of paper to complete your answer.

Here are some guidelines to remember when writing your open-ended answers:

- Organize your ideas and express them clearly.

- Correctly organize and separate your paragraphs.

- Support your ideas with examples when necessary.

- Make your writing interesting and enjoyable to read.

- Check your spelling and use of grammar and punctuation.

- Your answers should be accurate and complete.

THE PENDLETON ACT (1883)

In the years after the Civil War, the federal bureaucracy was generally undistinguished because the system of selecting officials and supervising their work was irrational. That system had evolved in the early nineteenth century. It relied on the well-known political adage, "To the victor belong the spoils." That did not necessarily mean that bad people were appointed; many government officials were quite good, but the system itself was ill-suited to efficiency.

The idea of rotation in office, however, was thought to be "democratic." In 1829, Andrew Jackson had declared, "No man has any more intrinsic right to official station than another . . . The duties of all public officers are, or at least admit of being made, so plain and simple that men of intelligence may readily qualify themselves for their performance." This neither true then nor true fifty years later.

Constant turnover became a problem. Government workers panicked at every election and had little sense of loyalty to their jobs, mainly because the length that they held those jobs was often so short. As Henry Clay put it, government officials after an election are "like the inhabitants of Cairo when the plague breaks out; no one knows who is next to encounter the stroke of death."

Over the years, the flaws became more serious and obvious. Political leaders required their patronage appointees to devote time and money to party affairs. After each election, winners were besieged by hungry office-seekers. Wrangling between the president and Congress over patronage became a large problem. By the 1880s, one could open a Washington newspaper after an election and find many advertisements like this one:

WANTED—A GOVERNMENT CLERKSHIP at a salary of not less than $1,000 per annum. Will give $100 to any one securing me such a position.

The situation was compounded by the growth of the federal bureaucracy. In Andrew Jackson's time, there had been 20,000 persons on the federal payroll. By end of the Civil War, the number had increased to 53,000; by 1884, 131,000; and by 1891, 166,000. Presidents were hounded by office-seekers. When James Garfield became president, he discovered hungry office-seekers "lying in wait" for him "like vultures for a wounded bison."

Moreover, new government jobs required special skills. The use of typewriters—introduced in the early 1880s—meant that mere literacy and decent penmanship were no longer enough to secure a clerk's job. With the creation of administrative agencies like the Interstate Commerce Commission and specialized agricultural bureaus, a person needed scientific expertise.

A civil service movement started in New York in 1877. Although it developed considerable public support, the politicians refused to follow along. When Charles Guiteau, a disappointed office-seeker, assassinated President Garfield, the public clamor could no longer be ignored.

The Pendleton Act classified certain jobs, removed them from the patronage ranks, and set up a Civil Service Commission to administer a system based on getting jobs because of merit rather than political connections. As the classified list was expanded over the years, it provided the American people with a competent and permanent government bureaucracy. In 1883, fewer than 15,000 jobs were classified. By the time William McKinley became president in 1897, 86,000—almost half of all federal employees—were in classified positions. Today, with the exception of a few thousand policy-level appointments, nearly all federal jobs are handled within the civil service system.

The Pendleton Act (1883)

An act to regulate and improve the civil service of the United States.

Be it enacted . . . That the President is authorized to appoint, by and with the advice and consent of the Senate, three persons, not more than two of whom shall be adherents of the same party, as Civil Service Commissioners, and said three commissioners shall constitute the United States Civil Service Commission. Said commissioners shall hold no other official place under the United States.

Sec. 2. That it shall be the duty of said commissioners:

First. To aid the President, as he may request, in preparing suitable rules for carrying this act into effect, and when said rules shall have been promulgated it shall be the duty of all officers of the United States in the departments and offices to which any such rules may relate to aid, in all proper ways, in carrying said rules, and any modifications thereof, into effect.

Second. And, among other things, said rules shall provide and declare, as nearly as the conditions of good administration will warrant, as follows:

First, for open, competitive examinations for testing the fitness of applicants for the public service now classified or to be classified hereunder. Such examinations shall be practical in their character, and so far as may be shall relate to those matters which will fairly test the relative capacity and fitness of the persons examined to discharge the duties of the service into which they seek to be appointed.

Second, that all the offices, places, and employments so arranged or to be arranged in classes shall be filled by selections according to grade from among those graded highest as the results of such competitive examinations.

Third, appointments to the public service aforesaid in the departmentsat Washington shall be apportioned among the several States and Territories and the District of Columbia upon the basis of population as ascertained at the last preceding census . . .

Fourth, that there shall be a period of probation before any absolute appointment or employment aforesaid.

Fifth, that no person in the public service is for that reason under any obligations to contribute to any political fund, or to render any political service, and that he will not be removed or otherwise prejudiced for refusing to do so.

Sixth, that no person in said service has any right to use his official authority or influence to coerce the political action of any person or body.

Seventh, there shall be non-competitive examinations in all proper cases before the commission, when competent persons do not compete, after notice has been given of the existence of the vacancy, under such rules as may be prescribed by the commissioners as to the manner of giving notice . . .

Sec. 8. That no person habitually using intoxicating beverages to excess shall be appointed to, or retained in, any office, appointment, or employment to which the provisions of this act are applicable.

Sec. 9. That whenever there are already two or more members of a family in the public service in the grades covered by this act, no other member of such family shall be eligible to appointment to grades.

Sec. 10. That no recommendation of any person who shall apply for office or place under the provisions of this act which may be given by any Senator or member of the House of Representatives, except as to the character or residence of the applicant, shall be received or considered by any person concerned in making any examination or appointment under this act.

Sec. 11. That no Senator, or Representative, or Territorial Delegate of the Congress, or Senator, Representative, or Delegate elect, or any officer or employee of either of said houses, and no executive, judicial, military, or naval officer of the United States, and no clerk or employee of any department, branch or bureau of the executive, judicial, or military or naval service of the United States, shall, directly or indirectly, solicit or receive, or be in any manner concerned in soliciting or receiving, any assessment, subscription, or contribution for any political purpose whatever, from any officer, clerk, or employee of the United States, or any department, branch, or bureau thereof, or from any person receiving any salary or compensation from moneys derived from the Treasury of the United States . . .

1. According to the document, how many Civil Service Commissioners can be of the same political party?

    A. 0
    B. 2
    C. 3
    D. 4

2. Who must consent to the appointment of Civil Service Commissioners?

    A. the vice president
    B. the Senate
    C. the House of Representatives
    D. prior Civil Service Commissioners

3. According to the document, which of the following people could **not** be considered for public office?

    A. a person who does not drink alcohol
    B. a person with a family member in public office
    C. a person recommended by a senator
    D. a person who refuses to contribute to a political fund

4. Whom do you think is the intended audience for the Pendleton Act? What does the act reveal about its audience? Use evidence from the document above to support your conclusion.

_____

_____

_____

_____

_____

_____

_____

_____

_____

_____

_____

_____

_____

_____

_____

_____

_____

_____

_____

_____

_____

_____

_____

_____

_____

YICK WO V. HOPKINS (1886)

Yick Wo v. Hopkins *was the first case where the United States Supreme Court ruled that a law which appeared to be race-neutral but was administered in a prejudicial manner was an infringement of the Equal Protection Clause in the Fourteenth Amendment to the U.S. Constitution.*

In the 1880s, Chinese immigrants to California faced many legal and economic hurdles, including discriminatory provisions in the California constitution. As a result, they were excluded—either by law or bias—from many professions. Many turned to the laundry business; in fact, in San Francisco, about 89 percent of the laundry workers were of Chinese descent.

In 1880, the city of San Francisco passed an ordinance that persons could not operate a laundry in a wooden building without a permit from the board of supervisors. At the time, about 95 percent of the city's 320 laundries were housed in wooden buildings. Approximately two-thirds of those laundries were owned by Chinese people. Although most of these people applied for a permit, none were granted to any Chinese owner. (Only one non-Chinese laundry owner was denied a permit.)

Yick Wo, who had lived in California and had operated a laundry in a wooden building for many years, continued to operate his laundry. He was convicted and fined $10 for violating the ordinance. He sued for a writ of habeas corpus *when he refused to pay the fine and was imprisoned for defaulting on the fine.*

The state argued that the ordinance was in place for safety reasons. All laundries needed very hot stoves to boil water to clean the clothes. In face, laundry fires were not uncommon; a fire of this type in an urban area would also often mean the destruction of adjoining buildings.

However, the petitioner pointed out that, prior to the new ordinance, the inspection and approval of laundries in wooden building had been left up to fire wardens. Yick Wo's laundry facility had never failed an inspection for fire safety. Moreover, the application of the prior law focused only on laundries in crowded areas of the city, while the new law was being enforced on isolated wooden buildings as well. The law also ignored other wooden buildings where fires were common.

The Supreme Court, in a unanimous opinion written by Justice Matthews, noted that it was clear that the administration of the law was discriminatory even if the ordinance was not. Even though the Chinese laundry owners were usually not American citizens, the court ruled that they were still entitled to equal protection under the Fourteenth Amendment. Matthews also noted that the court had previously ruled that it was acceptable to hold administrators of the law liable when they abused their authority. He denounced the law as a blatant attempt to exclude Chinese people from the laundry trade in San Francisco. The Supreme Court struck down the law, ordering dismissal of all charges against all other laundry owners who had been jailed.

Justice Matthews delivered the opinion of the court.

In the case of the petitioner, brought here by writ of error to the Supreme Court of California, our jurisdiction is limited to the question, whether the plaintiff in error has been denied a right in violation of the Constitution, laws, or treaties of the United States. . . .

We are consequently constrained, at the outset, to differ from the Supreme Court of California upon the real meaning of the ordinances in question. That court considered these ordinances as vesting in the board of supervisors a not unusual discretion in granting or withholding their assent to the use of wooden building as laundries, to be exercised in reference to the circumstances of each case, with a view to the protection of the public against the dangers of fire. We are not able to concur in that interpretation of the power conferred upon the supervisors. There is nothing in the ordinances which points to such a regulation of the business of keeping and conducting laundries. They seem intended to confer, and actually do confer, not a discretion to be exercised upon a consideration of the circumstances of each case, but a naked and arbitrary power to give or withhold consent, not only as to places, but as to persons. So that, if an applicant for such consent, being in every way a competent and qualified person, and having complied with every reasonable condition demanded by any public interest, should, failing to obtain the requisite consent of the supervisors to the prosecution of his business, apply for redress by the judicial process of mandamus, to require the supervisors to consider and act upon his case, it would be a sufficient answer for them to say that the law had conferred upon them authority to withhold their assent, without reason and without responsibility. The power given to them is not confided to their discretion in the legal sense of that term, but is granted to their mere will. It is purely arbitrary, and acknowledges neither guidance nor restraint. . . .

The ordinance drawn in question in the present case . . . does not prescribe a rule and conditions for the regulation of the use of property for laundry purposes, to which all similarly situated may conform. It allows without restriction the use for such purposes of buildings of brick or stone; but, as to wooden buildings, constituting nearly all those in previous use, it divides the owners or occupiers into two classes, not having respect to their personal character and qualifications for the business, nor the situation and nature and adaptation of the buildings themselves, but merely by an arbitrary line, on one side of which are those who are permitted to pursue their industry by the mere will and consent of the supervisors, and on the other those from whom that consent is withheld, at their mere will and pleasure. And both classes are alike only in this, that they are tenants at will, under the supervisors, of their means of living. The ordinance, therefore, also differs from the not unusual case, where discretion is lodged by law in public officers or bodies to grant or withhold licenses to keep taverns, or places for the sale of spirituous liquors, and the like, when one of the conditions is that the applicant shall be a fit person for the exercise of the privilege, because in such cases the fact of fitness is submitted to the judgement of the officer, and calls for the exercise of a discretion of a judicial nature.

The rights of the petitioners, as affected by the proceedings of which they complain, are not less, because they are aliens and subjects of the Emperor of China. . . .

The Fourteenth Amendment to the Constitution is not confined to the protection of citizens. It says: "Nor shall any State deprive any person of life, liberty, or property without due process of law; nor deny to any person within its jurisdiction the equal protection of the laws." These provisions are universal in their application, to all persons within the territorial jurisdiction, without regard to any differences of race, of color, or of nationality; and the equal protection of the laws is a pledge of the protection of equal laws. It is accordingly enacted by 1977 of the Revised Statutes, that "all persons within the jurisdiction of the United States shall have the same right in every State and Territory to make and enforce contracts, to sue, be parties, give evidence, and to the full and equal benefit of all law and proceedings for the security of persons and property as is enjoyed by white citizens and shall be subject to like punishment, pains, penalties, taxes, licenses, and exactions of every kind, and to no other." The questions we have to consider and decide in these cases, therefore, are to be treated as involving the rights of every citizen of the United States equally with those of the strangers and aliens who now invoke the jurisdiction of the court.

It is contended on the part of the petitioners, that the ordinances for violations of which they are severely sentenced to imprisonment, are void on their face, as being within the prohibitions of the Fourteenth Amendment; and in the alternative, if not so, that they are void by reason of their administration, operating unequally, so as to punish in the present petitioners what is permitted to others as lawful, without any distinction of circumstances—an unjust and illegal discrimination, it is claimed, which, though not made expressly by the ordinances is made possible by them. . . . to the actual, and pass upon the validity of the ordinances complained of, as tried merely by the opportunities which their terms afford, of unequal and unjust discrimination in their administration. For the cases present the ordinances in actual operation, and the facts shown establish an administration directed so exclusively against a particular class of persons as to warrant and require the conclusion, that, whatever may have been the intent of the ordinances as adopted, they are applied by the public authorities charged with their administration, and thus representing the State itself, with a mind so unequal and oppressive as to amount to the practical denial by the State of that equal protection of the laws which is secured to the petitioners, as to all other persons, by the broad and benign provisions of the Fourteenth Amendment to the Constitution of the United States. Though the law itself be fair on its face and impartial in appearance, yet, if it is applied and administered by public authority with an evil eye and an unequal hand, so as practically to make unjust and illegal discriminations between persons in similar circumstances, material to their rights, the denial of equal justice is still within the prohibition of the Constitution. . . .

The present cases, as shown by the facts disclosed in the record, are within this class. It appears that both petitioners have complied with every requisite, deemed by the law or by the public officers charged with its administration, necessary for the protection of neighboring property from fire, or as a precaution against injury to the public health. No reason whatever, except the will of the supervisors, is assigned why they should not be permitted to carry on, in the accustomed manner, their harmless and useful occupation, on which they depend for a livelihood. And while this consent of the supervisors is withheld from them and from two hundred others who have also petitioned, all of whom happen to be Chinese subjects, eighty others, not Chinese subjects, are permitted to carry on the same business under similar conditions. The fact of this discrimination is admitted. No reason for it is shown, and the conclusion cannot be resisted, that no reason for it exists except hostility to the race and nationality to which the petitioners belong, and which in the eye of the law is not justified. The discrimination is, therefore, illegal, and the public administration which enforces it is a denial of the equal protection of the laws and a violation of the Fourteenth Amendment of the Constitution. The imprisonment of the petitioners is, therefore, illegal, and they must be discharged.

1. The author of this passage quotes the Fourteen Amendment mainly because it

    A. states that cases should be decided individually.
    B. points out the differences between how citizens and "strangers and aliens" should be treated.
    C. doesn't discriminate against certain types of people.
    D. supports the idea that the Chinese laundry owners shouldn't have been granted permits.

2. According to the document, which of the following could be considered when deciding whether or not to grant or withhold a license?

    A. color
    B. nationality
    C. race
    D. territorial jurisdiction

3. The supervisors were concerned about laundries being operated in wooden buildings because

    A. wooden buildings are poorly ventilated.
    B. wooden buildings are poorly constructed.
    C. wood rots over time and is dangerous.
    D. wood burns quickly and easily.

4. Justice Matthews says that, in many cases, the supervisors based their decisions on

    A. character and qualifications.
    B. will and consent.
    C. situation and building.
    D. owners and occupiers.

5. Do you think citizens of the United States should have the same rights as immigrants who are not yet citizens? Why or why not?

8

PEOPLE'S PARTY PLATFORM (1896)

As a group, farmers did not share in the general prosperity of the latter half of the nineteenth century. They believed that they had been marked out as special victims of the new industrial system. Beginning in the 1870s, farmers attempted in a number of ways to mount an effective political campaign to rectify what they saw as the corruption of government and economic power; they attributed this corruption to big businesses and railroads. In fact, much of the farmers' plight was due to factors unrelated to industrialization, such as fluctuations in international markets for corn and wheat. But perceptions are often more important than reality, and American farmers believed that the democratic system of their forebears was being subverted.

The most successful of the agrarian political movements was the People's Party, or the Populist Party. After the 1892 presidential campaign, this party appears to have had the strength to become a potent force in American politics. This strength lay primarily in the southern and midwestern states—the agricultural heartland of the nation—although its leaders tried to reach out and attract eastern workers.

The People's Party platform of 1896 is notable for several reasons. First, it summed up two decades of farmers' resentment against a system that they believed ignored their needs and mercilessly exploited them. But it was not just big business to which they objected. The Populists worried that the alliance between business and government would destroy American democracy. The various proposals they put forward had two aims: to relieve economic pressure on agricultur and to restore democracy by eliminating what the Populists saw as the corrupt and corrupting alliance between business and government.

Although considered radical at the time, many of these proposals, such as the direct election of senators and the income tax, would move into the political mainstream and be adopted over the next few decades. The platform in many ways set the reform agenda of the country during the years prior to World War I.

The Populist Party disappeared after the election of 1896. It was absorbed for the most part into the Democratic Party.

The People's Party, assembled in National Convention, reaffirms its allegiance to the principles declared by the founders of the Republic, and also to the fundamental principles of just government as enunciated in the platform of the party in 1892.

We recognize that through the connivance of the present and preceding Administrations the country has reached a crisis in its National life, as predicted in our declaration four years ago, and that prompt and patriotic action is the supreme duty of the hour.

We realize that, while we have political independence, our financial and industrial independence is yet to be attained by restoring to our country the Constitutional control and exercise of the functions necessary to a people's government, which functions have been basely surrendered by our public servants to corporate monopolies. The influence of European moneychangers has been more potent in shaping legislation than the voice of the American people. Executive power and patronage have been used to corrupt our legislatures and defeat the will of the people, and plutocracy has thereby been enthroned upon the ruins of democracy. To restore the Government intended by the fathers, and for the welfare and prosperity of this and future generations, we demand the establishment of an economic and financial system which shall make us masters of our own affairs and independent of European control, by the adoption of the following declarations of principles:

The Finances

1. We demand a National money, safe and sound, issued by the General Government only, without the intervention of banks of issue, to be a full legal tender for all debts, public and private; a just, equitable, and efficient means of distribution, direct to the people, and through the lawful disbursements of the Government.

2. We demand the free and unrestricted coinage of silver and gold at the present legal ratio of 16 to 1, without waiting for the consent of foreign nations.

3. We demand that the volume of circulating medium be speedily increased to an amount sufficient to meet the demand of the business and population, and to restore the just level of prices of labor and production.

4. We denounce the sale of bonds and the increase of the public interest-bearing debt made by the present Administration as unnecessary and without authority of law, and demand that no more bonds be issued, except by specific act of Congress.

5. We demand such legislation as will prevent the demonetization of the lawful money of the United States by private contract.

6. We demand that the Government, in payment of its obligation, shall use its option as to the kind of lawful money in which they are to be paid, and we denounce the present and preceding Administrations for surrendering this option to the holders of Government obligations.

7. We demand a graduated income tax, to the end that aggregated wealth shall bear its just proportion of taxation, and we regard the recent decision of the Supreme Court relative to the income-tax as a misinterpretation of the Constitution and an invasion of the rightful powers of Congress over the subject of taxation.

8. We demand that postal savings-banks be established by the Government for the safe deposit of the savings of the people and to facilitate exchange.

Railroads and Telegraphs

1. Transportation being a means of exchange and a public necessity, the Government should own and operate the railroads in the interest of the people and on a non-partisan basis, to the end that all may be accorded the same treatment in transportation, and that the tyranny and political power now exercised by the great railroad corporations, which result in the impairment, if not the destruction of the political rights and personal liberties of the citizens, may be destroyed. Such ownership is to be accomplished gradually, in a manner consistent with sound public policy.

2. The interest of the United States in the public highways built with public moneys, and the proceeds of grants of land to the Pacific railroads, should never be alienated, mortgaged, or

sold, but guarded and protected for the general welfare, as provided by the laws organizing such railroads. The foreclosure of existing liens of the United States on these roads should at once follow default in the payment thereof by the debtor companies; and at the foreclosure sales of said roads the Government shall purchase the same, if it becomes necessary to protect its interests therein, or if they can be purchased at a reasonable price; and the Government shall operate said railroads as public highways for the benefit of the whole people, and not in the interest of the few, under suitable provisions for protection of life and property, giving to all transportation interests equal privileges and equal rates for fares and freight.

3. We denounce the present infamous schemes for refunding these debts, and demand that the laws now applicable thereto be executed and administered according to their intent and spirit.

4. The telegraph, like the Post Office system, being a necessity for the transmission of news, should be owned and operated by the Government in the interest of the people.

The Public Lands

1. True policy demands that the National and State legislation shall be such as will ultimately enable every prudent and industrious citizen to secure a home, and therefore the land should not be monopolized for speculative purposes. All lands now held by railroads and other corporations in excess of their actual needs should by lawful means be reclaimed by the Government and held for actual settlers only, and private land monopoly, as well as alien ownership, should be prohibited.

2. We condemn the land grant frauds by which the Pacific railroad companies have through the connivance of the Interior Department, robbed multitudes of bona-fide settlers of their homes and miners of their claims, and we demand legislation by Congress which will enforce the exemption of mineral land from such grants after as well before the patent.

3. We demand that bona-fide settlers on all public lands be granted free homes, as provided in the National Homestead Law, and that no exception be made in the case of Indian reservations when opened for settlement, and that all lands not now patented come under this demand.

The Referendum

We favor a system of direct legislation through the initiative and referendum, under proper Constitutional safeguards.

Direct Election of President and Senators by the People

We demand the election of President, Vice-President, and United States Senators by a direct vote of the people . . .

The Territories

We favor home rule in the Territories and the District of Columbia, and the early admission of the Territories as States.

Public Salaries

All public salaries should be made to correspond to the price of labor and its products.

Employment to Be Furnished by Government

In times of great industrial depression, idle labor should be employed on public works as far as practicable. . . .

1. Who did the People's Party believe was unfairly influencing the American government?

    A. Congress
    B. U.S. executives
    C. the president
    D. Europeans

2. According to the document, who should benefit from the proceeds of grants of land to the Pacific railroads?

    A. the United States Post Office
    B. private businesses
    C. the government
    D. the general public

3. The People's Party believed that they should be able to coin silver without

    A. paying a high cost.
    B. the president's approval.
    C. the consent of foreign nations.
    D. having to issue a bond.

4. According to the document, settlers on public land should be

    A. forced to pay fair taxes.
    B. granted free homes.
    C. made to live on reservations.
    D. granted help in farming.

5. Which of the following **best** describes the attitude of the People's Party?

    A. spiteful and violent
    B. insightful and flexible
    C. angry and insistent
    D. dismayed and confused

6. Which of the following was **not** a financial demand of the People's Party?

    A. passing legislation to present the demonetization of lawful money by private contract
    B. increasing the volume of circulating medium quickly to an amount that meets demand
    C. graduating income tax so that aggregated wealth bears a just proportion to taxation
    D. promoting the sale of interest-bearing bonds to increase public interest-bearing debt

12

7. Based on your reading of this document and what you know from history, do you think the People's Party was granted its demands? Why or why not? Use information from the document to support your answer.

_____

_____

_____

_____

_____

_____

_____

_____

_____

_____

_____

_____

_____

_____

_____

_____

_____

_____

_____

_____

_____

_____

_____

_____

_____

JOINT RESOLUTION TO PROVIDE FOR ANNEXING THE HAWAIIAN ISLANDS TO THE UNITED STATES (1898)

In the 1890s, the efforts of the Hawaiian people to preserve their national sovereignty and native heritage ran headlong into the unstoppable force of American expansionism. Throughout the 19th century, westerners—particularly Americans—came to dominate Hawaii's economy and politics. When Queen Liliuokalani assumed the throne in 1891 and tried to reassert the power of the throne and the will of native Hawaiians, she was deposed by a small group of American businessmen, with the support of the American diplomats and the U.S. Navy.

Although even President Grover Cleveland challenged the legitimacy of this takeover, it did stand. To a nation poised to take its place as a world power, the control of Hawaii, strategically located to serve as a mid-Pacific naval installation, seemed crucial. In 1898, with a naval base firmly established at Pearl Harbor, the United States officially annexed Hawaii.

Fifty-fifth Congress of the United States of America;

At the Second Session,

Begun and held at the City of Washington on Monday, the sixth day of December, one thousand eight hundred and ninety-seven.

Joint Resolution to provide for annexing the Hawaiian Islands to the United States.

Whereas, the Government of the Republic of Hawaii having, in due form, signified its consent, in the manner provided by its constitution, to cede absolutely and without reserve to the United States of America, all rights of sovereignty of whatsoever kind in and over the Hawaiian Islands and their dependencies, and also to cede and transfer to the United States, the absolute fee and ownership of all public, Government, or Crown lands, public buildings or edifices, ports, harbors, military equipment, and all other public property of every kind and description belonging to the Government of the Hawaiian Islands, together with every right and appurtenance thereunto appertaining: Therefore,

Resolved by the Senate and House of Representatives of the United States of America in Congress assembled, That said cession is accepted, ratified, and confirmed, and that the said Hawaiian Islands and their dependencies be, and they are hereby, annexed as a part of the territory of the United States and are subject to the sovereign dominion thereof, and that all and singular the property and rights hereinbefore mentioned are vested in the United States of America.

The existing laws of the United States relative to public lands shall not apply to such lands in the Hawaiian Islands; but the Congress of the United States shall enact special laws for their management and disposition: *Provided,* That all revenue from or proceeds of the same, except as regards such part thereof as may be used or occupied for the civil, military, or naval purposes of the United States, or may be assigned for the use of the local government, shall be used solely for the benefit of the inhabitants of the Hawaiian Islands for educational and other public purposes.

Until Congress shall provide for the government of such islands all the civil, judicial, and military powers exercised by the officers of the existing government in said islands shall be vested in such person or persons and shall be exercised in such manner as the President of the United states shall direct; and the President shall have power to remove said officers and fill the vacancies so occasioned.

The existing treaties of the Hawaiian Islands with foreign nations shall forthwith cease and determine, being replaced by such treaties as may exist, or as may be hereafter concluded, between the United States and such foreign nations. The municipal legislation of the Hawaiian Islands, not enacted for the fulfillment of the treaties so extinguished, and not inconsistent with this joint resolution nor contrary to the Constitution of the United States nor to any existing treaty of the United States, shall remain in force until the Congress of the United States shall otherwise determine.

Until legislation shall be enacted extending the United States customs laws and regulations to the Hawaiian Islands the existing customs relations of the Hawaiian Islands with the United States and other countries shall remain unchanged.

The public debt of the Republic of Hawaii, lawfully existing at the date of the passage of this joint resolution, including the amounts due to depositors in the Hawaiian Postal Savings Bank, is hereby assumed by the Government of the United States; but the liability of the United States in this regard shall in no case exceed four million dollars. So long, however, as the existing Government and the present commercial relations of the Hawaiian Islands are continued as hereinbefore, provided said Government shall continue to pay the interest on said debt.

There shall be no further immigration of Chinese into the Hawaiian Islands, except upon such conditions as are now or may hereafter be allowed by the laws of the United States; and no Chinese, by reason of anything herein contained, shall be allowed to enter the United States from the Hawaiian Islands.

Sec. 1. The President shall appoint five commissioners, at least two of whom shall be residents of the Hawaiian Islands, who shall, as soon as reasonably practicable, recommend to Congress such legislation concerning the Hawaiian Islands as they shall deem necessary or proper.

Sec. 2. That the commissioners hereinbefore provided for shall be appointed by the President, by and with the advice and consent of the Senate.

Sec. 3. That the sum of one hundred thousand dollars, or so much thereof as may be necessary, is hereby appropriated, out of any money in the Treasury not otherwise appropriated, and to be immediately available, to be expended at the discretion of the President of the United States of America, for the purpose of carrying this joint resolution into effect.

(Letter of protest from Queen Liliuokalani of Hawaii to the House of Representatives)

The House of Representatives of the United States:

I, Liliuokalani of Hawaii, named heir apparent on the 10th day of April, 1877, and proclaimed Queen of the Hawaiian Islands on the 29th day of January, 1891, do hereby earnestly and respectfully protest against the assertion of ownership by the United States of America of the so-called Hawaiian Crown Islands amounting to about one million acres and which are my property, and I especially protest against such assertion of ownership as a taking of property without due process of law and without just or other compensation.

Therefore, supplementing my protest of June 17, 1897, I call upon the President and the National Legislature and the People of the United States to do justice in this matter and to restore to me this property, the enjoyment of which is being withheld from me by your Government under what must be a misapprehension of my right and title.

Done at Washington, District of Columbia, United States of America, this nineteenth day of December, in the year one thousand eight hundred and ninety-eight.

1. The people of Hawaii transferred all of the following to the United States **except**

    A. ports.
    B. private funds.
    C. harbors.
    D. public funds.

2. After it became part of the United States, Hawaii's treaties with other countries were

    A. modified.
    B. enacted.
    C. ended.
    D. honored.

3. Who assumed Hawaii's public debt?

    A. Queen Liliuokalani
    B. Hawaiian citizens
    C. American citizens
    D. the U.S. government

4. You can tell from this document that the word, "annex," means

    A. persuade.
    B. conquer.
    C. seize.
    D. compromise.

5. According to the document, who was forbidden to immigrate to Hawaii after it became part of the United States?

    A. Americans
    B. Hawaiians living elsewhere
    C. the Chinese
    D. Hawaiian royalty

6. Do you think the United States was right or wrong in removing Queen Liliuokalani from her throne? Use details and information from the document to support your answer.

_____

_____

_____

_____

_____

_____

_____

_____

_____

_____

_____

_____

_____

_____

_____

_____

_____

_____

_____

_____

_____

_____

_____

PLATT AMENDMENT (1903)

At the end of the Spanish-American War in 1898, the United States found itself in control of several overseas territories, including Cuba. In April 1898, Senator Henry M. Teller of Colorado proposed an amendment to the United States' declaration of war against Spain. The declaration stated that the United States would not establish permanent control over Cuba. The Teller Amendment asserted that the United States "hereby disclaims any disposition of intention to exercise sovereignty, jurisdiction, or control over said island except for pacification thereof, and asserts its determination, when that is accomplished, to leave the government and control of the island to its people." The U.S. Senate adopted the amendment on April 19th.

Nonetheless, the occupation of Cuba by U.S. troops continued for several years after the war was over. Under the military governor, General Leonard Wood, a school system was organized, finances were set in order, and significant progress was made in eliminating yellow fever. In July 1900, the Constitutional Convention of Cuba started its deliberations and was notified that the U.S. Congress intended to attach an amendment to the Cuban Constitution. In 1901, Secretary of War Elihu Root drafted a set of articles as guidelines for future United States–Cuban relations. This set of articles became known as the Platt Amendment, after Senator Orville Platt of Connecticut, who presented it. Platt was a senator from 1879 to 1905; he had influenced the decision to annex Hawaii and occupy the Philippines. He sponsored the Platt Amendment as a rider attached to the Army Appropriations Bill of 1901. Cubans reluctantly included the amendment, which virtually made Cuba a U.S. protectorate, in their constitution. The Platt Amendment was also incorporated in a permanent treaty between the United States and Cuba.

The Platt Amendment stipulated the conditions for U.S. intervention in Cuban affairs and permitted the United States to lease or buy lands for the purpose of establishing naval bases (the main one was Guantánamo Bay) and coaling stations in Cuba. It barred Cuba from making a treaty that gave another nation power over its affairs, from going into debt, or from stopping the United States from imposing a sanitation program on the island. Specifically, Article III required that the government of Cuba consent to the right of the United States to intervene in Cuban affairs for

> *the preservation of Cuban independence, the maintenance of a government adequate for the protection of life, property, and individual liberty, and for discharging the obligations with respect to Cuba imposed by the Treaty of Paris on the United States, now to be assumed and undertaken by the Government of Cuba.*

The Platt Amendment supplied the terms under which the United States intervened in Cuban affairs in 1906, 1912, 1917, and 1920. By 1934, rising Cuban nationalism and widespread criticism of the Platt Amendment resulted in its repeal as part of Franklin D. Roosevelt's Good Neighbor policy toward Latin America. The United States, however, retained its lease on Guantánamo Bay, where a naval base was established.

Whereas the Congress of the United States of America, by an Act approved March 2, 1901, provided as follows:

Provided further, That in fulfillment of the declaration contained in the joint resolution approved April twentieth, eighteen hundred and ninety-eight, entitled "For the recognition of the independence of the people of Cuba, demanding that the Government of Spain relinquish its authority and government in the island of Cuba, and withdraw its land and naval forces from Cuba and Cuban waters, and directing the President of the United States to use the land and naval forces of the United States to carry these resolutions into effect," the President is hereby authorized to "leave the government and control of the island of Cuba to its people" so soon as a government shall have been established in said island under a constitution which, either as a part thereof or in an ordinance appended thereto, shall define the future relations of the United States with Cuba, substantially as follows:

"I. That the government of Cuba shall never enter into any treaty or other compact with any foreign power or powers which will impair or tend to impair the independence of Cuba, nor in any manner authorize or permit any foreign power or powers to obtain by colonization or for military or naval purposes or otherwise, lodgement in or control over any portion of said island."

"II. That said government shall not assume or contract any public debt, to pay the interest upon which, and to make reasonable sinking fund provision for the ultimate discharge of which, the ordinary revenues of the island, after defraying the current expenses of government shall be inadequate."

"III. That the government of Cuba consents that the United States may exercise the right to intervene for the preservation of Cuban independence, the maintenance of a government adequate for the protection of life, property, and individual liberty, and for discharging the obligations with respect to Cuba imposed by the treaty of Paris on the United States, now to be assumed and undertaken by the government of Cuba."

"IV. That all Acts of the United States in Cuba during its military occupancy thereof are ratified and validated, and all lawful rights acquired thereunder shall be maintained and protected."

"V. That the government of Cuba will execute, and as far as necessary extend, the plans already devised or other plans to be mutually agreed upon, for the sanitation of the cities of the island, to the end that a recurrence of epidemic and infectious diseases may be prevented, thereby assuring protection to the people and commerce of Cuba, as well as to the commerce of the southern ports of the United States and the people residing therein."

"VI. That the Isle of Pines shall be omitted from the proposed constitutional boundaries of Cuba, the title thereto being left to future adjustment by treaty."

"VII. That to enable the United States to maintain the independence of Cuba, and to protect the people thereof, as well as for its own defense, the government of Cuba will sell or lease to the United States lands necessary for coaling or naval stations at certain specified points to be agreed upon with the President of the United States."

"VIII. That by way of further assurance the government of Cuba will embody the foregoing provisions in a permanent treaty with the United States."

1. According to the document, who should have control of Cuba as soon as a government was established?

   A. the people of the United States
   B. the people of Cuba
   C. the government of Paris
   D. the government of Spain

2. The document says that Cuba will sell or lease land to the United States for

   A. military bases.
   B. naval stations.
   C. sanitation.
   D. colonization.

3. According to the document, which country should relinquish all control over Cuba?

   A. Spain
   B. France
   C. America
   D. Great Britain

4. According to the document, when should the United States intervene in Cuban affairs? Use details from the document to support your answer.

   _____

   _____

   _____

   _____

   _____

   _____

   _____

   _____

   _____

   _____

   _____

   _____

   _____

   _____

THEODORE ROOSEVELT'S COROLLARY TO THE MONROE DOCTRINE (1905)

European intervention in Latin America (see the Platt Amendment) resurfaced as an issue in U.S. foreign policy when European governments began to use force to pressure several Latin American countries to repay their debts. For example, British, German, and Italian gunboats blockaded Venezuela's ports in 1902 when the Venezuelan government defaulted on its debts to foreign bondholders. Many Americans worried that European intervention in Latin America would undermine their country's traditional dominance over the region.

To keep other powers out and ensure financial solvency, President Theodore Roosevelt issued his corollary. "Chronic wrongdoing . . . may in America, as elsewhere, ultimately require intervention by some civilized nation," he announced in his annual message to Congress in December 1904, "and in the Western Hemisphere the adherence of the United States to the Monroe Doctrine may force the United States, however reluctantly, in flagrant cases of such wrongdoing or impotence, to the exercise of an international police power."

Roosevelt tied his policy to the Monroe Doctrine, and it was also consistent with his foreign policy of "walk softly, but carry a big stick." Roosevelt stated that in keeping with the Monroe Doctrine, the United States was justified in exercising "international police power" to put an end to chronic unrest or wrongdoing in the Western Hemisphere. This so-called "Roosevelt Corollary" (a corollary is an extension of a previous idea) to the Monroe Doctrine contained a great irony. The Monroe Doctrine had been sought to prevent European intervention in the Western Hemisphere, but now the Roosevelt Corollary justified American intervention throughout the Western Hemisphere. In 1934, Franklin D. Roosevelt renounced interventionism and established his Good Neighbor policy within the Western Hemisphere.

In treating of our foreign policy and of the attitude that this great Nation should assume in the world at large, it is absolutely necessary to consider the Army and the Navy, and the Congress, through which the thought of the Nation finds its expression, should keep ever vividly in mind the fundamental fact that it is impossible to treat our foreign policy, whether this policy takes shape in the effort to secure justice for others or justice for ourselves, save as conditioned upon the attitude we are willing to take toward our Army, and especially toward our Navy. It is not merely unwise, it is contemptible, for a nation, as for an individual, to use high-sounding language to proclaim its purposes, or to take positions which are ridiculous if unsupported by potential force, and then to refuse to provide this force. If there is no intention of providing and keeping the force necessary to back up a strong attitude, then it is far better not to assume such an attitude.

The steady aim of this Nation, as of all enlightened nations, should be to strive to bring ever nearer the day when there shall prevail throughout the world the peace of justice. There are kinds of peace which are highly undesirable, which are in the long run as destructive as any war. Tyrants and oppressors have many times made a wilderness and called it peace. Many times peoples who were slothful or timid or shortsighted, who had been enervated by ease or by luxury, or misled by false teachings, have shrunk in unmanly fashion from doing duty that was stern and that needed self-sacrifice, and have sought to hide from their own minds their shortcomings, their ignoble motives, by calling them love of peace. The peace of tyrannous terror, the peace of craven weakness, the peace of injustice, all these should be shunned as we shun unrighteous war. The goal to set before us as a nation, the goal which should be set before all mankind, is the attainment of the peace of justice, of the peace which comes when each nation is not merely safe-guarded in its own rights, but scrupulously recognizes and performs its duty toward others. Generally peace tells for righteousness; but if there is conflict between the two, then our fealty is due first to the cause of righteousness. Unrighteous wars are common, and unrighteous peace is rare; but both should be shunned. The right of freedom and the responsibility for the exercise of that right can not be divorced. One of our great poets has well and finely said that freedom is not a gift that tarries long in the hands of cowards. Neither does it tarry long in the hands of those too slothful, too dishonest, or too unintelligent to exercise it. The eternal vigilance which is the price of liberty must be exercised, sometimes to guard against outside foes; although of course far more often to guard against our own selfish or thoughtless shortcomings.

If these self-evident truths are kept before us, and only if they are so kept before us, we shall have a clear idea of what our foreign policy in its larger aspects should be. It is our duty to remember that a nation has no more right to do injustice to another nation, strong or weak, than an individual has to do injustice to another individual; that the same moral law applies in one case as in the other. But we must also remember that it is as much the duty of the Nation to guard its own rights and its own interests as it is the duty of the individual so to do. Within the Nation the individual has now delegated this right to the State, that is, to the representative of all the individuals, and it is a maxim of the law that for every wrong there is a remedy. But in international law we have not advanced by any means as far as we have advanced in municipal law. There is as yet no judicial way of enforcing a right in international law. When one nation wrongs another or wrongs many others, there is no tribunal before which the wrongdoer can be brought. Either it is necessary supinely to acquiesce in the wrong, and thus put a premium upon brutality and aggression, or else it is necessary for the aggrieved nation valiantly to stand up for its rights. Until some method is devised by which there shall be a degree of international control over offending nations, it would be a wicked thing for the most civilized powers, for those with most sense of international obligations and with keenest and most generous appreciation of the difference between right and wrong, to disarm. If the great civilized nations of the present day should completely disarm, the result would mean an immediate recrudescence of barbarism in one form or another. Under any circumstances a sufficient armament would have to be kept up to serve the purposes of international police; and until international cohesion and the sense of international duties and rights are far more advanced than at present, a nation desirous both of securing respect for itself and of doing good to others must have a force adequate for the work which it feels is allotted to it as its part of the general world duty. Therefore it follows that a self-respecting, just, and far-seeing nation should on the one hand endeavor by every means to aid in the development of the various movements which tend to provide substitutes for war, which tend to render nations in their actions toward one another, and indeed toward their own peoples, more responsive to the general sentiment of humane and civilized mankind; and on the other hand that it should keep prepared, while scrupulously avoiding wrongdoing itself, to repel any wrong, and in exceptional cases to take action which in a more advanced stage of international relations would come under the head of the exercise of the international police. A great free people owes it to itself and to all mankind not to sink into helplessness before the powers of evil.

We are in every way endeavoring to help on, with cordial good will, every movement which will tend to bring us into more friendly relations with the rest of mankind. In pursuance of this policy I shall shortly lay before the Senate treaties of arbitration with all powers which are willing to enter into these treaties with us. It is not possible at this period of the world's development to agree to arbitrate all matters, but there are many matters of possible difference between us and other nations which can be thus arbitrated. Furthermore, at the request of the Interparliamentary Union, an eminent body composed of practical statesmen from all countries, I have asked the Powers to join with this Government in a second Hague conference, at which it is hoped that the work already so happily begun at The Hague may be carried some steps further toward completion. This carries out the desire expressed by the first Hague conference itself.

It is not true that the United States feels any land hunger or entertains any projects as regards the other nations of the Western Hemisphere save such as are for their welfare. All that this country desires is to see the neighboring countries stable, orderly, and prosperous. Any country whose people conduct themselves well can count upon our hearty friendship. If a nation shows that it knows how to act with reasonable efficiency and decency in social and political matters, if it keeps order and pays its obligations, it need fear no interference from the United States. Chronic wrongdoing, or an impotence which results in a general loosening of the ties of civilized society, may in America, as elsewhere, ultimately require intervention by some civilized nation, and in the Western Hemisphere the adherence of the United States to the Monroe Doctrine may force the United States, however reluctantly, in flagrant cases of such wrongdoing or impotence, to the exercise of an international police power. If every country washed by the Caribbean Sea would show the progress in stable and just civilization which with the aid of the Platt Amendment Cuba has shown since our troops left the island, and which so many of the republics in both Americas are constantly and brilliantly showing, all question of interference by this Nation with their affairs would be at an end. Our interests and those of our southern neighbors are in reality identical. They have great natural riches, and if within their borders the reign of law and justice obtains, prosperity is sure to come to them. While they thus obey the primary laws of civilized society they may rest assured that they will be treated by us in a spirit of cordial and helpful sympathy. We would interfere with them only in the last resort, and then only if it became evident that their inability or unwillingness to do justice at home and abroad had violated the rights of the United States or had invited foreign aggression to the detriment of the entire body of American nations. It is a mere truism to say that every nation, whether in America or anywhere else, which desires to maintain its freedom, its independence, must ultimately realize that the right of such independence can not be separated from the responsibility of making good use of it.

In asserting the Monroe Doctrine, in taking such steps as we have taken in regard to Cuba, Venezuela, and Panama, and in endeavoring to circumscribe the theater of war in the Far East, and to secure the open door in China, we have acted in our own interest as well as in the interest of humanity at large. There are, however, cases in which, while our own interests are not greatly involved, strong appeal is made to our sympathies. Ordinarily it is very much wiser and more useful for us to concern ourselves with striving for our own moral and material betterment here at home than to concern ourselves with trying to better the condition of things in other nations. We have plenty of sins of our own to war against, and under ordinary circumstances we can do more for the general uplifting of humanity by striving with heart and soul to put a stop to civic corruption, to brutal lawlessness and violent race prejudices here at home than by passing resolutions and wrongdoing elsewhere. Nevertheless there are occasional crimes committed on so vast a scale and of such peculiar horror as to make us doubt whether it is not our manifest duty to endeavor at least to show our disapproval of the deed and our sympathy with those who have suffered by it. The cases must be extreme in which such a course is justifiable. There must be no effort made to remove the mote from our brother's eye if we refuse to remove the beam from our own. But in extreme cases action may be justifiable and proper. What form the action shall take must depend upon the circumstances of the case; that is, upon the degree of the atrocity and upon our power to remedy it. The cases in which we could interfere by force of arms as we interfered to put a stop to intolerable conditions in Cuba are necessarily very few. Yet it is not to be expected that a people like ours, which in spite of certain very obvious shortcomings, nevertheless as a whole shows by its consistent practice its belief in the principles of civil and religious liberty and of orderly freedom, a people among whom even the worst crime, like the crime of lynching, is never more than sporadic, so that individuals and not classes are molested in their fundamental rights—it is inevitable that such a nation should desire eagerly to give expression to its horror on an occasion like that of the massacre of the Jews in Kishenef, or when it witnesses such systematic and long-extended cruelty and oppression as the cruelty and oppression of which the Armenians have been the victims, and which have won for them the indignant pity of the civilized world.

1. According to the document, in order to earn the friendship of the United States, a country needs to

   A. conduct itself well.
   B. pay financial tributes.
   C. sign international treaties.
   D. ask for assistance.

2. According to the document, unrighteous war is

   A. more common than unrighteous peace.
   B. much worse than unrighteous peace.
   C. singularly deserving of contempt.
   D. unusual throughout the world.

3. President Roosevelt sees a nation's actions and responsibilities as comparable to those of

   A. an individual.
   B. a corporation.
   C. an international alliance.
   D. a meeting of leaders.

4. International law is **not** as effective as municipal law because

   A. municipal laws were created centuries ago.
   B. there are no international elected officials.
   C. each country must act in its own self-interest.
   D. it is difficult to enforce rights internationally.

5. Eternal vigilance is needed primarily to

   A. observe the cost of freedom.
   B. negotiate international agreements.
   C. guard against outside foes.
   D. guard against one's own shortcomings.

6. According to the document, the most sound foreign policy decisions should be based on

   A. political understandings.
   B. cultural differences.
   C. self-evident truths.
   D. opinions and beliefs.

7. According to the document, what would result if all civilized nations disarmed?

    A. unrighteous war
    B. righteous peace
    C. barbarism
    D. self-determination

8. The form of international policing action should depend upon all of the following factors **except** the

    A. degree of the atrocity.
    B. power of the remedy.
    C. location of the country.
    D. willingness of the people.

9. What is the title of the eminent body of statesmen from all countries?

    A. the Hague Union
    B. the Interparliamentary Union
    C. the Platt Union
    D. the International Union

10. Theodore Roosevelt believed that having a strong attitude required

    A. agreement of all countries.
    B. backing of necessary force.
    C. proof of good intentions.
    D. communication with others.

11. The Monroe Doctrine had been asserted in all of the following places **except**

    A. Cuba.
    B. Venezuela.
    C. Panama.
    D. Uruguay.

12. What is the "peace of justice"? Do you agree with President Roosevelt's estimate of this kind of peace as compared to others? Use evidence from the document to support your conclusions.

16TH AMENDMENT TO THE U.S. CONSTITUTION: FEDERAL INCOME TAX (1913)

Far-reaching in its social and economic impact, the income tax amendment became part of the Constitution by a curious series of events, culminating in a bit of political maneuvering that went awry.

The financial requirements of the Civil War prompted the first American income tax in 1861. At first, Congress placed a flat three-percent tax on all incomes over $800. They later modified this principle to include a graduated tax. Congress repealed the income tax in 1872, but the concept did not disappear.

After the Civil War, the growing industrial and financial markets of the eastern United States generally prospered. Unfortunately, the farmers of the south and west suffered from low prices for their farm products, while at at the same time being forced to pay high prices for manufactured goods. Throughout the 1860s, 1870s, and 1880s, farmers formed such political organizations as the Grange, the Greenback Party, the National Farmers' Alliance, and the People's (Populist) Party (see People's Party Platform). All of these groups advocated many reforms considered radical for the times, including a graduated income tax.

In 1894, as part of a high tariff bill, Congress enacted a two-percent tax on income over $4,000. The tax was almost immediately struck down by a five-to-four decision of the Supreme Court, even though the court had upheld the constitutionality of the Civil War tax as recently as 1881. Although farm organizations denounced the court's decision as a prime example of the alliance of government and business against the farmer, a general return of prosperity around the turn of the century softened the demand for reform. Democratic Party Platforms under the leadership of three-time presidential candidate William Jennings Bryan, however, consistently included an income tax plank. The progressive wing of the Republican Party also supported the concept.

In 1909, progressives in Congress again attached a provision for an income tax to a tariff bill. Conservatives, hoping to kill the idea for good, proposed a constitutional amendment enacting such a tax; they believed an amendment would never receive ratification by three-fourths of the states. Much to their surprise, the amendment was ratified by one state legislature after another. On February 25, 1913, with the certification by Secretary of State Philander C. Knox, the 16th Amendment took effect. Yet, in 1913, due to generous exemptions and deductions, less than one percent of the population paid income taxes at the rate of only one percent of net income.

This document settled the constitutional question of how to tax income and, by so doing, effected dramatic changes in the American way of life.

Sixty-first Congress of the United States of America, At the First Session,

Begun and held at the City of Washington on Monday, the fifteenth day of March, one thousand nine hundred and nine.

Joint Resolution

Proposing an amendment to the Constitution of the United States.

Resolved by the Senate and House of Representatives of the United States of America in Congress assembled (two-thirds of each House concurring therein), That the following article is proposed as an amendment to the Constitution of the United States, which, when ratified by the legislature of three-fourths of the several States, shall be valid to all intents and purposes as a part of the Constitution:

"**ARTICLE XVI.** The Congress shall have power to lay and collect taxes on incomes, from whatever source derived, without apportionment among the several States, and without regard to any census or enumeration."

1. What portion of the states in the country had to ratify the amendment to make it part of the U.S. Constitution?

   A. 1/4
   B. 1/3
   C. 1/2
   D. 2/3

2. According to the document, Congress can tax income that comes from

   A. employment only.
   B. inheritance only.
   C. personal gifts.
   D. any source.

3. How do you think Americans felt at first about the 16th Amendment? Use details from the document to support your answer.

_____

_____

_____

_____

_____

_____

_____

_____

_____

_____

_____

_____

17TH AMENDMENT TO THE U.S. CONSTITUTION: DIRECT ELECTION OF U.S. SENATORS (1913)

The Constitution, as it was adopted in 1788, made the Senate an assembly where the states would have equal representation. Each state legislature would elect two senators to six-year terms. Late in the 19th century, some state legislatures deadlocked over the election of a senator when different parties controlled different houses. At the time, Senate vacancies could last months or years. In other cases, special interests or political machines gained control over the state legislature. Progressive reformers dismissed individuals elected by such legislatures as puppets and the Senate as a "millionaire's club" serving powerful private interests.

One Progressive response to these concerns was the "Oregon system," which utilized a state's primary election to identify the voters' choice for senator, while pledging all candidates for the state legislature to honor the primary's result. Over half of the states adopted the "Oregon system," but the 1912 Senate investigation of bribery and corruption in the election of Illinois Senator William Lorimer indicated that only a constitutional amendment mandating the direct election of senators by a state's citizenry would allay public demands for reform.

When the House of Representatives passed proposed amendments for the direct election of senators in 1910 and 1911, they included a "race rider," which was meant to bar federal intervention in cases of racial discrimination among voters. This would be done by vesting complete control of Senate elections in state governments. A substitute amendment by Senator Joseph L. Bristow of Kansas provided for the direct election of senators without the "race rider." It was adopted by the Senate on a close vote before the proposed constitutional amendment itself passed the Senate. Over a year later, the House accepted the change. On April 8, 1913, this resolution became the 17th Amendment.

Transcript of 17th Amendment to the U.S. Constitution: Direct Election of U.S. Senators (1913)

Sixty-second Congress of the United States of America; At the Second Session,

Begun and held at the City of Washington on Monday, the fourth day of December, one thousand nine hundred and eleven.

Joint Resolution

Proposing an amendment to the Constitution providing that Senators shall be elected by the people of the several States.

Resolved by the Senate and House of Representatives of the United States of America in Congress assembled (two-thirds of each House concurring therein), That in lieu of the first paragraph of section three of Article I of the Constitution of the United States, and in lieu of so much of paragraph two of the same section as relates to the filling of vacancies, the following be proposed as an amendment to the Constitution, which shall be valid to all intents and purposes as part of the Constitution when ratified by the legislatures of three-fourths of the States:

"The Senate of the United States shall be composed of two Senators from each State, elected by the people thereof, for six years; and each Senator shall have one vote. The electors in each State shall have the qualifications requisite for electors of the most numerous branch of the State legislatures.

"When vacancies happen in the representation of any State in the Senate, the executive authority of such State shall issue writs of election to fill such vacancies: *Provided*, That the legislature of any State may empower the executive thereof to make temporary appointments until the people fill the vacancies by election as the legislature may direct.

"This amendment shall not be so construed as to affect the election or term of any Senator chosen before it becomes valid as part of the Constitution."

1. According to this document, how many senators will be elected by each state?

   A. one
   B. two
   C. three
   D. four

2. If the 17th Amendment was ratified by three-fourths of the legislature, it would be considered

   A. a new international standard.
   B. a duty for all Americans.
   C. part of the Constitution.
   D. a work of federal intervention.

3. Senate vacancies are to be permanently filled by officials who are

   A. elected by the people.
   B. handpicked by the president.
   C. chosen by the federal government.
   D. chosen by the state government.

4. What term of office and vote count is each senator to be given?

   A. one-year term and two votes
   B. two-year term and two votes
   C. four-year term and one vote
   D. six-year term and one vote

4. How are vacancies in the Senate filled? Use details and information from the document to support your answer.

_____

_____

_____

_____

_____

_____

_____

_____

_____

_____

_____

_____

_____

_____

_____

_____

_____

_____

_____

_____

_____

_____

_____

_____

_____

_____

31

KEATING-OWEN CHILD LABOR ACT OF 1916

The 1900 census revealed that approximately two million children were working in mills, mines, fields, factories, stores, and on city streets across the United States. The census report helped spark a national movement to end child labor in the United States. In 1908, the National Child Labor Committee hired Lewis Hine as its staff photographer. The organization sent him across the country to photograph and report on child labor. Social reformers began to condemn child labor because of its detrimental effects on the health and welfare of children. Among those helping to incite public opinion against it were Karl Marx and Charles Dickens, the latter of whom had worked at a factory himself at age twelve. One of the most effective attacks came from Dickens's novel, Oliver Twist, which was widely read in Britain and the United States. Dickens's masterwork portrays an orphan boy, raised in poorhouses and workhouses and by street criminals in industrialized London in the 1850s.

The first child labor bill—the Keating-Owen Bill of 1916—was based on Senator Albert J. Beveridge's proposal from 1906. The bill used the government's ability to regulate interstate commerce to similarly regulate child labor. The act banned the sale of products from any factory, shop, or cannery that employed children under the age of fourteen, from any mine that employed children under the age of sixteen, and from any facility that had children under the age of sixteen working at night or for more than eight hours during the day. Although the Keating-Owen Act was passed by Congress and signed into law by President Woodrow Wilson, the Supreme Court ruled that it was unconstitutional because it overstepped the purpose of the government's powers to regulate interstate commerce.

A second child labor bill was passed in December 1918. It also took an indirect route to regulate child labor, this time by using the government's power to levy taxes. It too was soon found to be unconstitutional in Hammer v. Dagenhart 247 U.S. 251 (1918). The Supreme Court reasoned, "The power of Congress to regulate interstate commerce does not extend to curbing the power of the states to regulate local trade."

Despite the nation's apparent desire for federal laws against child labor, the Supreme Court's rulings left little room for federal legislation. A constitutional amendment was soon proposed to give Congress the power to regulate child labor. The campaign for ratification of the Child Labor Amendment was stalled in the 1920s by an effective campaign to discredit it. Opponents' charges ranged from traditional states' rights arguments against increases in the power of the federal government to accusations that the amendment was a communist-inspired plot to subvert the Constitution.

Federal protection of children would not be obtained until passage of the Fair Labor Standards Act in 1938, which was also challenged before the Supreme Court. This time, the movement to end child labor was victorious. In February 1941, the Supreme Court reversed its opinion in Hammer v. Dagenhart and, in U.S. v. Darby (1941), upheld the constitutionality of the Fair Labor Standards Act. It is still in force today.

Sixty-fourth Congress of the United States of America; At the First Session,

Begun and held at the City of Washington on Monday, the sixth day of December, one thousand nine hundred and fifteen.

AN ACT To prevent interstate commerce in the products of child labor, and for other purposes.

Be it enacted by the Senate and House of Representatives of the United States of America in Congress assembled, That no producer, manufacturer, or dealer shall ship or deliver for shipment in interstate or foreign commerce, any article or commodity the product of any mine or quarry situated in the United States, in which within thirty days prior to the time of the removal of such product therefrom children under the age of sixteen years have been employed or permitted to work, or any article or commodity the product of any mill, cannery, workshop, factory, or manufacturing establishment, situated in the United States, in which within thirty days prior to the removal of such product therefrom children under the age of fourteen years have been employed or permitted to work, or children between the ages of fourteen years and sixteen years have been employed or permitted to work more than eight hours in any day, or more than six days in any week, or after the hour of seven o'clock postmeridian, or before the hour of six o'clock antemeridian: *Provided,* That a prosecution and conviction of a defendant for the shipment or delivery for shipment of any article or commodity under the conditions herein prohibited shall be a bar to any further prosecution against the same defendant for shipments or deliveries for shipment of any such article or commodity before the beginning of said prosecution.

SEC. 2. That the Attorney General, the Secretary of Commerce and the Secretary of Labor shall constitute a board to make and publish from time to time uniform rules and regulations for carrying out the provisions of this Act.

SEC. 3. That for the purpose of securing proper enforcement of this Act the Secretary of Labor, or any person duly authorized by him, shall have authority to enter and inspect at any time mines quarries, mills, canneries, workshops, factories, manufacturing establishments, and other places in which goods are produced or held for interstate commerce; and the Secretary of Labor shall have authority to employ such assistance for the purposes of this Act as may from time to time be authorized by appropriation or other law.

SEC. 4. That it shall be the duty of each district attorney to whom the Secretary of Labor shall report any violation of this Act, or to whom any State factory or mining or quarry inspector, commissioner of labor, State medical inspector or school-attendance officer, or any other person shall present satisfactory evidence of any such violation to cause appropriate proceedings to be commenced and prosecuted in the proper courts of the United States without delay for the enforcement of the penalties in such cases herein provided: *Provided,* That nothing in this Act shall be construed to apply to bona fide boys' and girls' canning clubs recognized by the Agricultural Department of the several States and of the United States.

SEC. 5. That any person who violates any of the provisions of section one of this Act, or who refuses or obstructs entry or inspection authorized by section three of this Act, shall for each offense prior to the first conviction of such person under the provisions of this Act, be punished by a fine of not more than $200, and shall for each offense subsequent to such conviction be punished by a fine of not more than $1,000, nor less than $100, or by imprisonment for not more than three months, or by both such fine and imprisonment, in the discretion of the court: *Provided,* That no dealer shall be prosecuted under the provisions of this Act for a shipment, delivery for shipment, or transportation who establishes a guaranty issued by the person by whom the goods shipped or delivered for shipment or transportation were manufactured or produced, resident in the United States, to the effect that such goods were produced or manufactured in a mine or quarry in which within thirty days prior to their removal therefrom no children under the age of sixteen years were employed or permitted to work, or in a mill, cannery, workshop, factory, or manufacturing establishment in which within thirty days prior to the removal of such goods therefrom no children under the ages of fourteen years were employed or permitted to work, nor children between the ages of fourteen years and sixteen years employed or permitted to work more than eight hours in any day or more than six days in any week or after the hour of seven o'clock postmeridian o before the hour of six o'clock antemeridian; and in such event, if the guaranty contains any false statement or a material fact the guarantor shall be amenable to prosecution and to the fine or imprisonment provided by this section for violation of the provisions of this Act. Said guaranty, to afford the protection above provided, shall contain the name and address of the person giving the same: And provided further, That no producer, manufacturer, or dealer shall be prosecuted under this Act for the shipment, delivery for shipment, or transportation of a product of any mine, quarry, mill, cannery, workshop, factory, or manufacturing establishment, if the only employment therein within thirty days prior to the removal of such product therefrom, of a child under the age of sixteen years has been that of a child as to whom the producer, or manufacturer has in; good faith procured, at the time of employing such child, and has since in good faith relied upon and kept on file a certificate, issued in such form, under such conditions, any by such persons as may be prescribed by the board, showing the child to be of such an age that the shipment, delivery for shipment, or transportation was not prohibited by this Act. Any person who knowingly makes a false statement or presents false evidence in or in relation to any such certificate or application therefor shall be amenable to prosecution and to the fine or imprisonment provided by this section for violations of this Act. In any State designated by the board, an employment certificate or other similar paper as to the age of the child, issued under the laws of that State and not inconsistent with the provisions of this Act, shall have the same force and effect as a certificate herein provided for.

SEC. 6. That the word "person" as used in this Act shall be construed to include any individual or corporation or the members of any partnership or other unincorporated association. The term "ship or deliver for shipment in interstate or foreign commerce" as used in this Act means to transport or to ship or deliver for shipment from any State or Territory or the District of Columbia to or through any other State or Territory or the District of Columbia or to any foreign country; and in the case of a dealer means only to transport or to ship or deliver for shipment from the State, Territory or district of manufacture or production.

SEC. 7. That this Act shall take effect from and after one year from the date of its passage.

Approved, September 1, 1916.

1. According to the document, who may at any time inspect premises of businesses to make sure child labor laws are being followed?

    A. the Secretary of Labor
    B. the U.S. District Attorney
    C. the Secretary of State
    D. the U.S. Attorney General

2. The document says that all of the following are illegal **except**

   A. employing a child under age 14.
   B. employing a child who is age 15.
   C. permitting a 16-year-old to work five days a week.
   D. permitting a 16-year-old to work nine hours a day.

3. Which of the following is excluded from the act discussed in this document?

   A. boys' canning clubs
   B. mines
   C. quarries
   D. manufacturing establishments

4. Which of the following might be a fine for a first-time violation of the Keating-Owen Child Labor Act?

   A. $150
   B. $201
   C. $500
   D. $1,000

5. The document says that all of the following should be on a board to publish rules about child labor **except** the

   A. U.S. Attorney General.
   B. Secretary of Labor.
   C. U.S. District Attorney.
   D. Secretary of Commerce.

6. When did this act go into effect?

   A. immediately
   B. one day from the date it was passed
   C. one month from the date it was passed
   D. one year from the date it was passed

7. Do you think children under age 16 should be allowed to work for pay? Use details from the document to support your answer.

_____

_____

_____

_____

_____

_____

_____

_____

_____

_____

_____

_____

_____

_____

_____

_____

_____

_____

_____

_____

_____

_____

ZIMMERMANN TELEGRAM (1917)

Between 1914 and the spring of 1917, the European nations engaged in a conflict that became known as World War I. While armies battled in Europe, the United States remained neutral. In 1916, Woodrow Wilson was elected president for a second term, largely because of the slogan, "He kept us out of war." Events in early 1917 changed that sentiment.

In January 1917, British cryptographers deciphered a telegram from German Foreign Minister Arthur Zimmermann to the German Minister to Mexico, von Eckhardt, offering United States territory to Mexico in return for joining the German cause. To protect their intelligence from detection and to capitalize on growing anti-German sentiment in the United States, the British waited to present the telegram to President Wilson. Meanwhile, frustration over the effective British naval blockade caused Germany to break its pledge to limit submarine warfare. In response, the United States severed diplomatic relations with Germany in February.

On February 24th, Britain released the Zimmermann Telegram to Wilson. News of the telegram was published widely in the American press on March 1st. The telegram had such an impact on American opinion that, according to David Kahn, author of The Codebreakers, *"No other single cryptanalysis has had such enormous consequences." It is his opinion that "never before or since has so much turned upon the solution of a secret message." On April 6, 1917, the United States Congress formally declared war on Germany and its allies. The Zimmermann Telegram clearly helped draw the United States into the war and thus changed the course of history.*

FROM 2nd from London #5747.

"We intend to begin on the first of February unrestricted submarine warfare. We shall endeavor in spite of this to keep the United States of America neutral. In the event of this not succeeding, we make Mexico a proposal or alliance on the following basis: make war together, make peace together, generous financial support and an understanding on our part that Mexico is to reconquer the lost territory in Texas, New Mexico, and Arizona. The settlement in detail is left to you. You will inform the President of the above most secretly as soon as the outbreak of war with the United States of America is certain and add the suggestion that he should, on his own initiative, invite Japan to immediate adherence and at the same time mediate between Japan and ourselves. Please call the President's attention to the fact that the ruthless employment of our submarines now offers the prospect of compelling England in a few months to make peace." Signed, ZIMMERMANN.

1. What type of warfare did the Germans plan to increase?

   A. land
   B. plane
   C. ship
   D. submarine

2. According to the document, Mexico planned to reconquer all of the following **except**

   A. Texas.
   B. California.
   C. New Mexico.
   D. Arizona.

3. Zimmermann would have preferred that the United States remain

   A. aligned with Germany.
   B. against Germany.
   C. on no particular side.
   D. in support of Mexico.

4. Which of the following **best** describes Zimmermann's tone?

   A. independent and ruthless
   B. generous and concerned
   C. strategic and unemotional
   D. manipulative and spiteful

5. What message does Zimmermann give to Mexico? Use details and information from the document to support your answer.

_____

_____

_____

_____

_____

_____

_____

_____

_____

_____

_____

_____

_____

_____

_____

JOINT ADDRESS TO CONGRESS LEADING TO A DECLARATION OF WAR AGAINST GERMANY (1917)

Hostilities broke out between several nations of Europe in 1914. Almost immediately, President Wilson declared America's intent to stay neutral and called on all Americans to remain impartial to the war in thought and deed. However, Wilson and the United States found it increasingly difficult to remain neutral. The series of events between 1915 and 1917 led Wilson to finally deliver his war message to Congress on April 2, 1917.

German submarine warfare had resulted in the sinking of several ships and the loss of American lives. Most remarkable was the attack against the Lusitania, *on May 7, 1915, when 128 Americans died. While that ship flew the American flag of neutrality, it also carried several thousand cases of ammunition and shrapnel headed to Great Britain. After stern warnings from Wilson, the Germans pledged to abide by traditional rules of search and seizure. Increasingly, however, America was drawn to the side of the British. In addition to historic cultural ties to both Britain and France, munitions shipments to those countries from the United States had increased from around $6 million in 1914 to almost $500 million in 1917. American bankers had also loaned the Allies over $2 billion.*

On the heels of the German announcement to renew unrestricted submarine warfare on February 1, 1917, the British, on February 24th, revealed the Zimmerman Telegram. When Wilson released the message to the press on March 1st, Americans were shocked and angered. With the support of his entire cabinet, Wilson—who had been reelected in 1916 on the slogan, "He kept us out of war"— reluctantly concluded that war was inevitable. In his speech before a special session of Congress, Wilson took the moral high ground and declared that not only had America's rights as a neutral country been violated but that "The world must be made safe for democracy." He said that Americans had to fight "for the rights and liberties of small nations" and to "bring peace and safety to make the world itself at last free."

ADDRESS:

GENTLEMEN OF THE CONGRESS:

I have called the Congress into extraordinary session because there are serious, very serious, choices of policy to be made, and made immediately, which it was neither right nor constitutionally permissible that I should assume the responsibility of making.

On the third of February last I officially laid before you the extraordinary announcement of the Imperial German Government that on and after the first day of February it was its purpose to put aside all restraints of law or of humanity and use its submarines to sink every vessel that sought to approach either the ports of Great Britain and Ireland or the western coasts of Europe or any of the ports controlled by the enemies of Germany within the Mediterranean. That had seemed to be the object of the German submarine warfare earlier in the war, but since April of last year the Imperial Government had somewhat restrained the commanders of its undersea craft in conformity with its promise then given to us that passenger boats should not be sunk and that due warning would be given to all other vessels which its submarines might seek to destroy when no resistance was offered or escape attempted, and care taken that their crews were given at least a fair chance to save their lives in their open boats. The precautions taken were meager and haphazard enough, as was proved in distressing instance after instance in the progress of the cruel and unmanly business, but a certain degree of restraint was observed. The new policy has swept every restriction aside. Vessels of every kind, whatever their flag, their character, their cargo, their destination, their errand, have been ruthlessly sent to the bottom: without warning and without thought of help or mercy for those on board, the vessels of friendly neutrals along with those of belligerents. Even hospital ships and ships carrying relief to the sorely bereaved and stricken people of Belgium, though the latter were provided with safe conduct through the proscribed areas by the German Government itself and were distinguished by unmistakable marks of identity, have been sunk with the same reckless lack of compassion or of principle. I was for a little while unable to believe that such things would in fact be done by any government that had hitherto subscribed to the humane practices of civilized nations. International law had its origin in the attempt to set up some law which would be respected and observed upon the seas, where no nation had right of dominion and where lay the free highways of the world. . . . This minimum of right the German Government has swept aside under the plea of retaliation and necessity and because it had no weapons which it could use at sea except these which it is impossible to employ as it is employing them without throwing to the winds all scruples of humanity or of respect for the understandings that were supposed to underlie the intercourse of the world. I am not now thinking of the loss of property involved, immense and serious as that is, but only of the wanton and wholesale destruction of the lives of noncombatants, men, women, and children, engaged in pursuits which have always, even in the darkest periods of modern history, been deemed innocent and legitimate. Property can be paid for; the lives of peaceful and innocent people cannot be. The present German submarine warfare against commerce is a warfare against mankind.

It is a war against all nations. American ships have been sunk, American lives taken, in ways which it has stirred us very deeply to learn of, but the ships and people of other neutral and friendly nations have been sunk and overwhelmed in the waters in the same way. There has been no discrimination. The challenge is to all mankind. Each nation must decide for itself how it will meet it. The choice we make for ourselves must be made with a moderation of counsel and a temperateness of judgment befitting our character and our motives as a nation. We must put excited feeling away. Our motive will not be revenge or the victorious assertion of the physical might of the nation, but only the vindication of right, of human right, of which we are only a single champion.

When I addressed the Congress on the twenty-sixth of February last I thought that it would suffice to assert our neutral rights with arms, our right to use the seas against unlawful interference, our right to keep our people safe against unlawful violence. But armed neutrality, it now appears, is impracticable. Because submarines are in effect outlaws when used as the German submarines have been used against merchant shipping, it is impossible to defend ships against their attacks as the law of nations has assumed that merchantmen would defend themselves against privateers or cruisers, visible craft giving chase upon the open sea. It is common prudence in such circumstances, grim necessity indeed, to endeavor to destroy them before they have shown their own intention. They must be dealt with upon sight, if dealt with at all. The German Government denies the right of neutrals to use arms at all within the areas of the sea which it has proscribed, even in the defense of rights which no modern publicist has ever before questioned their right to defend. The intimation is conveyed that the armed guards which we have placed on our merchant ships will be treated as beyond the pale of law and subject to be dealt with as pirates would be. Armed neutrality is ineffectual enough at best; in such circumstances and in the face of such pretensions it is worse than ineffectual: it is likely only to produce what it was meant to prevent; it is practically certain to draw us into the war without either the rights or the effectiveness of belligerents. There is one choice we cannot make, we are incapable of making: we will not choose the path of submission and suffer the most sacred rights of our Nation and our people to be ignored or violated. The wrongs against which we now array ourselves are no common wrongs; they cut to the very roots of human life.

40

With a profound sense of the solemn and even tragical character of the step I am taking and of the grave responsibilities which it involves, but in unhesitating obedience to what I deem my constitutional duty, I advise that the Congress declare the recent course of the Imperial German Government to be in fact nothing less than war against the government and people of the United States; that it formally accept the status of belligerent which has thus been thrust upon it, and that it take immediate steps not only to put the country in a more thorough state of defense but also to exert all its power and employ all its resources to bring the Government of the German Empire to terms and end the war.

What this will involve is clear. It will involve the utmost practicable cooperation in counsel and action with the governments now at war with Germany, and, as incident to that, the extension to those governments of the most liberal financial credit, in order that our resources may so far as possible be added to theirs. It will involve the organization and mobilization of all the material resources of the country to supply the materials of war and serve the incidental needs of the Nation in the most abundant and yet the most economical and efficient way possible. It will involve the immediate full equipment of the navy in all respects but particularly in supplying it with the best means of dealing with the enemy's submarines. It will involve the immediate addition to the armed forces of the United States already provided for by law in case of war at least five hundred thousand men, who should, in my opinion, be chosen upon the principle of universal liability to service, and also the authorization of subsequent additional increments of equal force so soon as they may be needed and can be handled in training. It will involve also, of course, the granting of adequate credits to the Government, sustained, I hope, so far as they can equitably be sustained by the present generation, by well conceived taxation. I say sustained so far as may be equitable by taxation because it seems to me that it would be most unwise to base the credits which will now be necessary entirely on money borrowed. It is our duty, I most respectfully urge, to protect our people so far as we may against the very serious hardships and evils which would be likely to arise out of the inflation which would be produced by vast loans.

In carrying out the measures by which these things are to be accomplished we should keep constantly in mind the wisdom of interfering as little as possible in our own preparation and in the equipment of our own military forces with the duty—for it will be a very practical duty—of supplying the nations already at war with Germany with the materials which they can obtain only from us or by our assistance. They are in the field and we should help them in every way to be effective there.

I shall take the liberty of suggesting, through the several executive departments of the Government, for the consideration of your committees, measures for the accomplishment of the several objects I have mentioned. I hope that it will be your pleasure to deal with them as having been framed after very careful thought by the branch of the Government upon which the responsibility of conducting the war and safeguarding the Nation will most directly fall.

While we do these things, these deeply momentous things, let us be very clear, and make very clear to all the world what our motives and our objects are. My own thought has not been driven from its habitual and normal course by the unhappy events of the last two months, and I do not believe that the thought of the Nation has been altered or clouded by them. I have exactly the same things in mind now that I had in mind when I addressed the Senate on the twenty-second of January last, the same that I had in mind when I addressed the Congress on the third of February and on the twenty-sixth of February. Our object now, as then, is to vindicate the principles of peace and justice in the life of the world as against selfish and autocratic power and to set up amongst the really free and selfgoverned peoples of the world such a concert of purpose and of action as will henceforth insure the observance of those principles Neutrality is no longer feasible or desirable where the peace of the world is involved and the freedom of its peoples, and the menace to that peace and freedom lies in the existence of autocratic governments backed by organized force which is controlled wholly by their will, not by the will of their people. We have seen the last of neutrality in such circumstances. We are at the beginning of an age in which it will be insisted that the same standards of conduct and of responsibility for wrong done shall be observed among nations and their governments that are observed among the individual citizens of civilized states.

We have no quarrel with the German people. We have no feeling towards them but one of sympathy and friendship. It was not upon their impulse that their government acted in entering this war. It was not with their previous knowledge or approval. It was a war determined upon as wars used to be determined upon in the old, unhappy days when peoples were nowhere consulted by their rulers and wars were provoked and waged in the interest of dynasties or of little groups of ambitious men who were accustomed to use their fellow men as pawns and tools.

Selfgoverned nations do not fill their neighbor states with spies or set the course of intrigue to bring about some critical posture of affairs which will give them an opportunity to strike and make conquest. Such designs can be successfully worked out only under cover and where no one has the right to ask questions. Cunningly contrived plans of deception or aggression, carried, it may be, from generation to generation, can be worked out and kept from the light only within the privacy of courts or behind the carefully guarded confidences of a narrow and privileged class. They are happily impossible where public opinion commands and insists upon full information concerning all the nation's affairs.

A steadfast concert for peace can never be maintained except by a partnership of democratic nations. No autocratic government could be trusted to keep faith within it or observe its covenants. It must be a league of honor, a partnership of opinion. Intrigue would eat its vitals away; the plottings of inner circles who could plan what they would and render account to no one would be a corruption seated at its very heart. Only free peonies can hold their purpose and their honor steady to a common end and prefer the interests of mankind to any narrow interest of their own.

Does not every American feel that assurance has been added to our hope for the future peace of the world by the wonderful and heartening things that have been happening within the last few weeks in Russia? Russia was known by those who knew it best to have been always in fact democratic at heart, in all the vital habits of her thought, in all the intimate relationships of her people that spoke their natural instinct, their habitual attitude towards life. The autocracy that crowned the summit of her political structure, long as it had stood and terrible as was the reality of its power, was not in fact Russian in origin, character, or purpose; and now it has been shaken off and the great, generous Russian people have been added in all their naive majesty and might to the forces that are fighting for freedom in the world, for justice, and for peace. Here is a fit partner for a League of Honor.

One of the things that has served to convince us that the Prussian, autocracy was not and could never be our friend is that from the very outset of the present war it has filled our unsuspecting communities and even our offices of government with spies and set criminal intrigues everywhere afoot against our national unity of counsel, our peace Within and without, our industries and our commerce. Indeed it is now evident that its spies were here even before the war began; and it is unhappily not a matter of conjecture but a fact proved in our courts of justice that the intrigues which have more than once come perilously near to disturbing the peace and dislocating the industries of the country have been carried on at the instigation, with the support, and even under the personal direction of official agents of the Imperial Government accredited to the Government of the United States. Even in checking these things and trying to extirpate them we have sought to put the most generous interpretation possible upon them because we knew that their source lay, not in any hostile feeling or purpose of the German people towards us (who were, no doubt, as ignorant of them as we ourselves were), but only in the selfish designs of a Government that did what it pleased and told its people nothing. But they have played their part in serving to convince us at last that that Government entertains no real friendship for us and means to act against our peace and security at its convenience. That it means to stir up enemies against us at our very doors the intercepted note to the German Minister at Mexico City is eloquent evidence.

We are accepting this challenge of hostile purpose because we know that in such a Government, following such methods, we can never have a friend; and that in the presence of its organized power, always lying in wait to accomplish we know not what purpose, there can be no assured security for the democratic Governments of the world. We are now about to accept gauge of battle with this natural foe to liberty and shall, if necessary, spend the whole force of the nation to check and nullify its pretensions and its power. We are glad, now that we see the facts with no veil of false pretense about them to fight thus for the ultimate peace of the world and for the liberation of its peoples, the German peoples included: for the rights of nations great and small and the privilege of men everywhere to choose their way of life and of obedience. The world must be made safe for democracy. Its peace must be planted upon the tested foundations of political liberty. We have no selfish ends to serve.

We desire no conquest, no dominion. We seek no indemnities for ourselves, no material compensation for the sacrifices we shall freely make. We are but one of the champions of the rights of mankind. We shall be satisfied when those rights have been made as secure as the faith and the freedom of nations can make them. Just because we fight without rancor and without selfish object, seeking nothing for ourselves but what we shall wish to share with all free peoples, we shall, I feel confident, conduct our operations as belligerents without passion and ourselves observe with proud punctilio the principles of right and of fair play we profess to be fighting for.

I have said nothing of the Governments allied with the Imperial Government of Germany because they have not made war upon us or challenged us to defend our right and our honor. The Austro-Hungarian Government has, indeed, avowed its unqualified endorsement and acceptance of the reckless and lawless submarine warfare adopted now without disguise by the Imperial German Government, and it has therefore not been possible for this Government to receive Count Tarnowski, the Ambassador recently accredited to this Government by the Imperial and Royal Government of Austria-Hungary; but that Government has not actually engaged in warfare against citizens of the United States on the seas, and I take the liberty, for the present at least, of postponing a discussion of our relations with the authorities at Vienna. We enter this war only where we are clearly forced into it because there are no other means of defending our rights.

It will be all the easier for us to conduct ourselves as belligerents in a high spirit of right and fairness because we act without animus, not in enmity towards a people or with the desire to bring any injury or disadvantage upon them, but only in armed opposition to an irresponsible government which has thrown aside all considerations of humanity and of right and is running amuck. We are, let me say again, the sincere friends of the German people, and shall desire nothing so much as the early reestablishment of intimate relations of mutual advantage between us,—however hard it may be for them, for the time being, to believe that this is spoken from our hearts. We have borne with their present Government through all these bitter months because of that friendship,—exercising a patience and forbearance which would otherwise have been impossible. We shall, happily, still have an opportunity to prove that friendship in our daily attitude and actions towards the millions of men and women of German birth and native sympathy who live amongst us and share our life, and we shall be proud to prove it towards all who are in fact loyal to their neighbors and to the Government in the hour of test. They are, most of them, as true and loyal Americans as if they had never known any other fealty or allegiance. They will be prompt to stand with us in rebuking and restraining the few who may be of a different mind and purpose. If there should be disloyalty, it will be dealt with with a firm hand of stern repression; but, if it lifts its head at all, it will lift it only here and there and without countenance except from a lawless and malignant few.

43

It is a distressing and oppressive duty, Gentlemen of the Congress, which I have performed in thus addressing you. There are, it may be many months of fiery trial and sacrifice ahead of us. It is a fearful thing to lead this great peaceful people into war, into the most terrible and disastrous of all wars, civilization itself seeming to be in the balance.

But the right is more precious than peace, and we shall fight for the things which we have always carried nearest our hearts,—for democracy, for the right of those who submit to authority to have a voice in their own Governments, for the rights and liberties of small nations, for a universal dominion of right by such a concert of free peoples as shall bring peace and safety to all nations and make the world itself at last free. To such a task we can dedicate our lives and our fortunes, every thing that we are and everything that we have, with the pride of those who know that the day has come when America is privileged to spend her blood and her might for the principles that gave her birth and happiness and the peace which she has treasured. God helping her, she can do no other.

1. President Wilson believed that Germany filled America with

   A. disloyalty to alliances.
   B. fear of going to war.
   C. overwhelming patriotism.
   D. criminal intrigues.

2. Wilson viewed Germany's submarine attacks as

   A. national safeguard.
   B. eloquent evidence.
   C. nullified pretensions.
   D. warfare against mankind.

3. According to President Wilson, the aim of the German submarine campaign was to

   A. enrage the Allied nations.
   B. provoke a war with America.
   C. intimidate England into submission.
   D. sink all vessels near enemy ports.

4. Continuous German aggression destroyed all hope of

   A. victory.
   B. neutrality.
   C. naval superiority.
   D. world peace.

5. The German submarine attacks were seen by America as acts of

   A. diplomacy.
   B. war.
   C. desperation.
   D. piracy.

6. In light of recent events, Wilson believed that Russia was

   A. unstable and dangerous.
   B. suited for autocracy.
   C. democratic at heart.
   D. a potential enemy.

7. America's declaration of war against Germany would involve all of the following **except**

   A. deploying the navy.
   B. planting spies in Germany.
   C. expanding the army.
   D. raising taxes.

8. According to this document, blame for the note sent to the German Minister at Mexico City lay with

   A. German soldiers.
   B. German rulers.
   C. the German people.
   D. the German culture.

9. President Wilson felt that supplying materials to Germany's enemies was

   A. too risky.
   B. too costly.
   C. unnecessary.
   D. practical.

10. Why did President Wilson believe that democracy was needed for lasting peace? How did Germany fail to meet this standard?

_____

_____

_____

_____

_____

_____

_____

_____

_____

_____

_____

19TH AMENDMENT TO THE CONSTITUTION: WOMEN'S RIGHT TO VOTE (1920)

The 19th Amendment guarantees all American women the right to vote. Achieving this milestone required a lengthy and difficult struggle. Victory took decades of agitation and protest. Beginning in the mid-19th century, several generations of women's suffrage supporters lectured, wrote, marched, lobbied, and practiced civil disobedience to achieve what many Americans considered a radical change of the Constitution. Few early supporters lived to see final victory in 1920.

Beginning in the 1800s, women organized, petitioned, and picketed to win the right to vote, but it took them decades to accomplish their purpose. The amendment was first introduced in Congress in 1878. On August 18, 1920, it was ratified. In that 42-year span of time, champions of voting rights for women worked tirelessly, but strategies for achieving their goal varied. Some pursued a strategy of passing suffrage acts in each state; nine western states adopted woman suffrage legislation by 1912. Others challenged male-only voting laws in the courts. Militant suffragists used tactics such as parades, silent vigils, and hunger strikes. Often, supporters met fierce resistance. Opponents heckled, jailed, and sometimes physically abused them.

By 1916, almost all of the major suffrage organizations were united behind the goal of a constitutional amendment. When New York adopted women's suffrage in 1917 and President Wilson changed his position to support an amendment in 1918, the political balance began to shift.

On May 21, 1919, the House of Representatives passed the amendment. Two weeks later, the Senate followed. When Tennessee became the 36th state to ratify the amendment on August 18, 1920, the amendment passed its final hurdle of obtaining the agreement of three-fourths of the states. Secretary of State Bainbridge Colby certified the ratification on August 26, 1920, changing the face of the American electorate forever.

Sixty-sixth Congress of the United States of America; At the First Session,

Begun and held at the City of Washington on Monday, the nineteenth day of May, one thousand nine hundred and nineteen.

JOINT RESOLUTION

Proposing an amendment to the Constitution extending the right of suffrage to women.

Resolved by the Senate and House of Representatives of the United States of America in Congress assembled (two-thirds of each House concurring therein), That the following article is proposed as an amendment to the Constitution, which shall be valid to all intents and purposes as part of the Constitution when ratified by the legislature of three-fourths of the several States.

"ARTICLE———.

"The right of citizens of the United States to vote shall not be denied or abridged by the United States or by any State on account of sex.

Congress shall have power to enforce this article by appropriate legislation."

1. The document says that this amendment will be enforced by

    A. retribution.
    B. force.
    C. legislation.
    D. cooperation.

2. You can tell from this document that the word, "suffrage," means the right to

    A. vote.
    B. support.
    C. fairness.
    D. public office.

3. Do you think that giving women the right to vote changed the outcomes of many elections? Why or why not? Use details and information from the document to support your answer.

_____

_____

_____

_____

_____

_____

_____

_____

_____

_____

_____

_____

_____

_____

_____

_____

_____

_____

NATIONAL INDUSTRIAL RECOVERY ACT (1933)

The National Industrial Recovery Act (NIRA) was enacted by Congress in June 1933 and was one of the measures by which President Franklin D. Roosevelt sought to assist the nation's economic recovery during the Great Depression. The passage of NIRA ushered in a unique experiment in U.S. economic history. The NIRA sanctioned, supported, and in some cases, enforced an alliance of industries. Antitrust laws were suspended. Companies were required to write industry-wide "codes of fair competition" that effectively fixed prices and wages, established production quotas, and imposed restrictions on entry of other companies into the alliances. The act further called for industrial self-regulation and declared that codes of fair competition—for the protection of consumers, competitors, and employers—were to be drafted for the various industries of the country. These codes were to be subject to public hearings. Employees were given the right to organize and bargain collectively. As a condition of employment, employees could not be told not to join or refrain from joining a labor organization.

The National Recovery Administration (NRA), created by a separate executive order, was put into operation soon after the final approval of the act. President Roosevelt appointed Hugh S. Johnson as administrator for industrial recovery. The administration was empowered to make voluntary agreements dealing with hours of work, rates of pay, and the fixing of prices. Until March 1934, the NRA was engaged chiefly in drawing up these industrial codes for all industries to adopt. More than 500 codes of fair practice were adopted for the various industries. Patriotic appeals were made to the public, and firms were asked to display the Blue Eagle, an emblem signifying NRA participation.

From the beginning, the NRA reflected divergent goals and suffered from widespread criticism. The businessmen who dominated the code-drafting wanted guaranteed profits. They insisted on security for their renewed investment and future production. Congressional critics insisted on continued open pricing and saw the NRA codes as a necessary means of making it fair and orderly. A few intellectuals wanted an even more extensive government role in the form of central economic planning. Finally, unhappy labor union representatives fought with little success for the collective bargaining promised by the NIRA. The codes did little to help recovery; in fact, by raising prices, they actually made the economic situation worse.

Though under criticism from all sides, the NRA did not last long enough to fully implement its policies. In May 1935, in the case of the Schechter Poultry Corp. v. *United States, the U.S. Supreme Court invalidated the compulsory-code system on the grounds that the NRA improperly delegated legislative powers to the executive and that the provisions of the poultry code (in the case in question) did not constitute a regulation of interstate commerce*

In a lengthy and unanimous opinion, the court seemed to demonstrate a complete unwillingness to endorse Franklin Roosevelt's argument that the national crisis of economic depression demanded radical innovation. Later, FDR would use this court opinion as evidence that the court was living in the "horse and buggy" era and needed to be reformed.

AN ACT

To encourage national industrial recovery, to foster fair competition, and to provide for the construction of certain useful public works, and for other purposes.

Be it enacted by the Senate and House of Representatives of the United States of America in Congress assembled,

TITLE I – INDUSTRIAL RECOVERY

DECLARATION OF POLICY

SECTION 1. A national emergency productive of widespread unemployment and disorganization of industry, which burdens interstate and foreign commerce, affects the public welfare, and undermines the standards of living of the American people, is hereby declared to exist. It is hereby declared to be the policy of Congress to remove obstructions to the free flow of interstate and foreign commerce which tend to diminish the amount thereof; and to provide for the general welfare by promoting the organization of industry for the purpose of cooperative action among trade groups, to induce and maintain united action of labor and management under adequate governmental sanctions and supervision, to eliminate unfair competitive practices, to promote the fullest possible utilization of the present productive capacity of industries, to avoid undue restriction of production (except as may be temporarily required), to increase the consumption of Industrial and agricultural products by increasing purchasing power, to reduce and relieve unemployment, to improve standards of labor, and otherwise to rehabilitate industry and to conserve natural resources.

ADMINISTRATIVE AGENCIES

SEC. 2. (a) To effectuate the policy of this title, the President is hereby authorized to establish such agencies, to accept and utilize such voluntary and uncompensated services to appoint without regard to the provisions of the civil service laws, such officers and employees, an to utilize such Federal officers and employees, and, with the consent of the State, such State and local officers and employees, as he may find necessary, to prescribe their authorities, duties, responsibilities, and tenure, and, without regard to the Classification Act of 1923, as amended, to fix the compensation of any officers and employees so appointed.

(b) The President may delegate any of his functions and powers under this title to such officers, agents, and employees as lie may designate or appoint, and may establish an industrial planning and research agency to aid in carrying out his functions under this title.

(c) This title shall cease to be in effect and any agencies established hereunder shall cease to exist at the expiration of two years after the date of enactment of this Act, or sooner if the President shall by proclamation or the Congress shall by joint resolution declare that the emergency recognized by section 1 has ended. . . .

1. The main purpose of the National Industrial Recovery Act was to

    A. foster business expansion.
    B. improve the standard of living.
    C. increase trade.
    D. change values.

2. How long would the title last if the president and Congress did not declare that the emergency had ended?

    A. 1 year
    B. 2 years
    C. 4 years
    D. 10 years

3. According to the document, unemployment and disorganized industries affect all of the following **except**

    A. foreign commerce.
    B. rate of immigration.
    C. standard of living.
    D. public welfare.

4. Do you agree with Franklin Roosevelt that the Supreme Court was living in the "horse and buggy" era? Why or why not?

    _____

    _____

    _____

    _____

    _____

    _____

    _____

    _____

    _____

    _____

    _____

    _____

    _____

    _____

    _____

    _____

    _____

50

NATIONAL LABOR RELATIONS ACT (1935)

After the National Industrial Recovery Act was declared unconstitutional by the Supreme Court, organized labor was again looking for relief from employers who had been free to spy on, interrogate, discipline, discharge, and blacklist union members. In the 1930s, workers had begun to organize militantly. In 1933 and 1934, a great wave of strikes occurred across the nation in the form of citywide general strikes and factory takeovers. Violent confrontations occurred between workers trying to form unions and the police and private security forces defending the interests of anti-union employers.

In a Congress sympathetic to labor unions, the National Labor Relations Act (NLRA) was passed in July 1935. The broad intention of the act—commonly known as the Wagner Act after Senator Robert R. Wagner of New York—was to guarantee employees "the right to self-organization, to form, join, or assist labor organizations, to bargain collectively through representatives of their own choosing, and to engage in concerted activities for the purpose of collective bargaining or other mutual aid and protection." The NLRA applied to all employers involved in interstate commerce except airlines, railroads, agriculture, and government.

In order to enforce and maintain those rights, the act included provisions for the National Labor Relations Board (NLRB) to arbitrate deadlocked labor-management disputes, guarantee democratic union elections, and penalize unfair labor practices by employers. To this day, the board of five members, appointed by the president, is assisted by 33 regional directors. The NLRB further determines proper bargaining units, conducts elections for union representation, and investigates charges of unfair labor practices by employers. Unfair practices, by law, include such things as interference, coercion, or restraint in labor's self-organizing rights; interference with the formation of labor unions; encouragement or discouragement of union membership; and the refusal to bargain collectively with a duly chosen employee representatives.

The constitutionality of the NLRA was upheld by the United States Supreme Court in National Labor Relations Board *v.* Jones & Laughlin Steel Corp. *in 1937. The act contributed to a dramatic surge in union membership and made labor a force to be reckoned with both politically and economically. Women benefited from this shift to unionization as well. By the end of the 1930s, 800,000 women belonged to unions, a threefold increase from 1929. The provisions of the NLRA were later expanded under the Taft-Hartley Labor Act of 1957 and the Landrum-Griffin Act of 1959.*

AN ACT To diminish the causes of labor disputes burdening or obstructing interstate and foreign commerce, to create a National Labor Relations Board, and for other purposes.

FINDINGS AND POLICIES

Section 1. The denial by some employers of the right of employees to organize and the refusal by some employers to accept the procedure of collective bargaining lead to strikes and other forms of industrial strife or unrest, which have the intent or the necessary effect of burdening or obstructing commerce by (a) impairing the efficiency, safety, or operation of the instrumentalities of commerce; (b) occurring in the current of commerce; (c) materially affecting, restraining, or controlling the flow of raw materials or manufactured or processed goods from or into the channels of commerce, or the prices of such materials or goods in commerce; or (d) causing diminution of employment and wages in such volume as substantially to impair or disrupt the market for goods flowing from or into the channels of commerce.

The inequality of bargaining power between employees who do not possess full freedom of association or actual liberty of contract and employers who are organized in the corporate or other forms of ownership association substantially burdens and affects the flow of commerce, and tends to aggravate recurrent business depressions, by depressing wage rates and the purchasing power of wage earners in industry and by preventing the stabilization of competitive wage rates and working conditions within and between industries.

Experience has proved that protection by law of the right of employees to organize and bargain collectively safeguards commerce from injury, impairment, or interruption, and promotes the flow of commerce by removing certain recognized sources of industrial strife and unrest, by encouraging practices fundamental to the friendly adjustment of industrial disputes arising out of differences as to wages, hours, or other working conditions, and by restoring equality of bargaining power between employers and employees.

Experience has further demonstrated that certain practices by some labor organizations, their officers, and members have the intent or the necessary effect of burdening or obstructing commerce by preventing the free flow of goods in such commerce through strikes and other forms of industrial unrest or through concerted activities which impair the interest of the public in the free flow of such commerce. The elimination of such practices is a necessary condition to the assurance of the rights herein guaranteed

It is declared to be the policy of the United States to eliminate the causes of certain substantial obstructions to the free flow of commerce and to mitigate and eliminate these obstructions when they have occurred by encouraging the practice and procedure of collective bargaining and by protecting the exercise by workers of full freedom of association, self-organization, and designation of representatives of their own choosing, for the purpose of negotiating the terms and conditions of their employment or other mutual aid or protection . . .

1. Which of the following is **not** an employer activity that causes workers to strike?

    A. not allowing workers to organize
    B. maintaining unfair wages
    C. negotiating contracts
    D. ignoring collective bargaining

2. Labor disputes are harmful to industries primarily because they

    A. obstruct commerce.
    B. shake workers' confidence.
    C. promote lawlessness.
    D. raise unemployment rates.

3. Unfair labor practices can aggravate business depressions by

    A. giving advantages to companies overseas.
    B. working employees into exhaustion.
    C. encouraging employers to outsource more jobs.
    D. lowering wages and purchasing power.

4. How does this document define labor strikes? Do you think strikes are an effective means of negotiation?

_____

_____

_____

_____

_____

_____

_____

_____

_____

_____

_____

_____

_____

_____

_____

_____

_____

_____

_____

_____

_____

_____

_____

_____

_____

PRESIDENT FRANKLIN ROOSEVELT'S RADIO ADDRESS UNVEILING THE SECOND HALF OF THE NEW DEAL (1936)

In this campaign speech delivered at Madison Square Garden on October 31, 1936, Roosevelt responded to considerable criticism that the New Deal had not done enough by emphasizing his administration's continuing plans for relief, reform, and recovery. Historians have often referred to this initiative as the Second New Deal. The major legislation that came out of the so-called Second New Deal was the Works Progress Administration (WPA), the National Labor Relations (Wagner) Act, the Social Security Act, and the Wealth Tax Act. The Wealth Tax Act brought about a sudden increase in taxes on the wealthy. It also created new and larger taxes on excess business profits, inheritances, large gifts, and profits from the sale of property.

The Works Progress (later "Work Projects") Administration promoted both relief and reform. The WPA built streets, highways, bridges, airfields, and post offices and other pubic buildings and facilities; restored forests; developed parks and recreation areas; built reservoirs; and extended electrical power to rural areas. Over its seven-year history, the WPA employed about 8.5 million Americans.

In addition to developing America's infrastructure, the WPA worked to promote American culture. The Federal Theater, Arts, Music, Dance, and Writers' Projects brought music and drama to even the smallest communities; sponsored public sculptures and murals; and commissioned noted American writers such as John Steinbeck, Richard Wright, John Cheever, and Claude McKay to write regional guidebooks and histories of the American people. This was the first time that the federal government had taken any responsibility for supporting and promoting American art and culture.

Within a week of the delivery of this speech, FDR was reelected to a second term as president of the United States. In the presidential campaign of 1936, Roosevelt led the Democratic Party in building what came to be called the "Roosevelt Coalition." While Republicans were still relying on their traditional support base (big business, big farmers, and conservatives), the Democrats—armed with FDR's Second New Deal—broadened their base of support by appealing to small farmers of the midwest, urban political bosses, ethnic blue-collar workers, Jews, intellectuals, African Americans, and Southern Democrats. The most dramatic shift to the Democratic Party was seen in the voting patterns of African Americans.

The Republican Party nominated Alfred M. Landon, the relatively liberal governor of Kansas, to oppose Roosevelt. Despite all the complaints leveled at the New Deal, Roosevelt won an even more decisive victory than in 1932. He took 60 percent of the popular vote, with a winning margin of 10 million votes, and carried every state except Maine and Vermont. The campaign speech shown here reflects FDR's continued commitment to economic reform for an America still suffering from the pains of the Great Depression.

Campaign Address at Madison Square Garden, New York City. "We Have Only Just Begun to Fight." October 31, 1936

Senator Wagner, Governor Lehman, ladies and gentlemen:

ON THE eve of a national election, it is well for us to stop for a moment and analyze calmly and without prejudice the effect on our Nation of a victory by either of the major political parties.

The problem of the electorate is far deeper, far more vital than the continuance in the Presidency of any individual. For the greater issue goes beyond units of humanity—it goes to humanity itself.

In 1932 the issue was the restoration of American democracy; and the American people were in a mood to win. They did win. In 1936 the issue is the preservation of their victory. Again they are in a mood to win. Again they will win.

More than four years ago in accepting the Democratic nomination in Chicago, I said: "Give me your help not to win votes alone, but to win in this crusade to restore America to its own people."

The banners of that crusade still fly in the van of a Nation that is on the march.

It is needless to repeat the details of the program which this Administration has been hammering out on the anvils of experience. No amount of misrepresentation or statistical contortion can conceal or blur or smear that record. Neither the attacks of unscrupulous enemies nor the exaggerations of over-zealous friends will serve to mislead the American people.

What was our hope in 1932? Above all other things the American people wanted peace. They wanted peace of mind instead of gnawing fear.

First, they sought escape from the personal terror which had stalked them for three years. They wanted the peace that comes from security in their homes: safety for their savings, permanence in their jobs, a fair profit from their enterprise.

Next, they wanted peace in the community, the peace that springs from the ability to meet the needs of community life: schools, playgrounds, parks, sanitation, highways—those things which are expected of solvent local government. They sought escape from disintegration and bankruptcy in local and state affairs.

They also sought peace within the Nation: protection of their currency, fairer wages, the ending of long hours of toil, the abolition of child labor, the elimination of wild-cat speculation, the safety of their children from kidnappers.

And, finally, they sought peace with other Nations—peace in a world of unrest. The Nation knows that I hate war, and I know that the Nation hates war.

I submit to you a record of peace; and on that record a well-founded expectation for future peace—peace for the individual, peace for the community, peace for the Nation, and peace with the world.

Tonight I call the roll—the roll of honor of those who stood with us in 1932 and still stand with us today.

Written on it are the names of millions who never had a chance—men at starvation wages, women in sweatshops, children at looms.

Written on it are the names of those who despaired, young men and young women for whom opportunity had become a will-o'-the-wisp.

Written on it are the names of farmers whose acres yielded only bitterness, business men whose books were portents of disaster, home owners who were faced with eviction, frugal citizens whose savings were insecure.

Written there in large letters are the names of countless other Americans of all parties and all faiths, Americans who had eyes to see and hearts to understand, whose consciences were burdened because too many of their fellows were burdened, who looked on these things four years ago and said, "This can be changed. We will change it."

We still lead that army in 1936. They stood with us then because in 1932 they believed. They stand with us today because in 1936 they know. And with them stand millions of new recruits who have come to know.

Their hopes have become our record.

We have not come this far without a struggle and I assure you we cannot go further without a struggle.

For twelve years this Nation was afflicted with hear-nothing, see-nothing, do-nothing Government. The Nation looked to Government but the Government looked away. Nine mocking years with the golden calf and three long years of the scourge! Nine crazy years at the ticker and three long years in the breadlines! Nine mad years of mirage and three long years of despair! Powerful influences strive today to restore that kind of government with its doctrine that that Government is best which is most indifferent.

For nearly four years you have had an Administration which instead of twirling its thumbs has rolled up its sleeves. We will keep our sleeves rolled up.

We had to struggle with the old enemies of peace—business and financial monopoly, speculation, reckless banking, class antagonism, sectionalism, war profiteering.

They had begun to consider the Government of the United States as a mere appendage to their own affairs. We know now that Government by organized money is just as dangerous as Government by organized mob.

Never before in all our history have these forces been so united against one candidate as they stand today. They are unanimous in their hate for me—and I welcome their hatred.

I should like to have it said of my first Administration that in it the forces of selfishness and of lust for power met their match. I should like to have it said of my second Administration that in it these forces met their master.

The American people know from a four-year record that today there is only one entrance to the White House—by the front door. Since March 4, 1933, there has been only one pass-key to the White House. I have carried that key in my pocket. It is there tonight. So long as I am President, it will remain in my pocket.

Those who used to have pass-keys are not happy. Some of them are desperate. Only desperate men with their backs to the wall would descend so far below the level of decent citizenship as to foster the current pay-envelope campaign against America's working people. Only reckless men, heedless of consequences, would risk the disruption of the hope for a new peace between worker and employer by returning to the tactics of the labor spy.

Here is an amazing paradox! The very employers and politicians and publishers who talk most loudly of class antagonism and the destruction of the American system now undermine that system by this attempt to coerce the votes of the wage earners of this country. It is the 1936 version of the old threat to close down the factory or the office if a particular candidate does not win. It is an old strategy of tyrants to delude their victims into fighting their battles for them.

Every message in a pay envelope, even if it is the truth, is a command to vote according to the will of the employer. But this propaganda is worse—it is deceit.

They tell the worker his wage will be reduced by a contribution to some vague form of old-age insurance. They carefully conceal from him the fact that for every dollar of premium he pays for that insurance, the employer pays another dollar. That omission is deceit.

They carefully conceal from him the fact that under the federal law, he receives another insurance policy to help him if he loses his job, and that the premium of that policy is paid 100 percent by the employer and not one cent by the worker. They do not tell him that the insurance policy that is bought for him is far more favorable to him than any policy that any private insurance company could afford to issue. That omission is deceit.

They imply to him that he pays all the cost of both forms of insurance. They carefully conceal from him the fact that for every dollar put up by him his employer puts up three dollars—three for one. And that omission is deceit.

But they are guilty of more than deceit. When they imply that the reserves thus created against both these policies will be stolen by some future Congress, diverted to some wholly foreign purpose, they attack the integrity and honor of American Government itself. Those who suggest that, are already aliens to the spirit of American democracy. Let them emigrate and try their lot under some foreign flag in which they have more confidence.

The fraudulent nature of this attempt is well shown by the record of votes on the passage of the Social Security Act. In addition to an overwhelming majority of Democrats in both Houses, seventy-seven Republican Representatives voted for it and only eighteen against it and fifteen Republican Senators voted for it and only five against it. Where does this last-minute drive of the Republican leadership leave these Republican Representatives and Senators who helped enact this law?

I am sure the vast majority of law-abiding businessmen who are not parties to this propaganda fully appreciate the extent of the threat to honest business contained in this coercion.

I have expressed indignation at this form of campaigning and I am confident that the overwhelming majority of employers, workers and the general public share that indignation and will show it at the polls on Tuesday next.

Aside from this phase of it, I prefer to remember this campaign not as bitter but only as hard-fought. There should be no bitterness or hate where the sole thought is the welfare of the United States of America. No man can occupy the office of President without realizing that he is President of all the people.

It is because I have sought to think in terms of the whole Nation that I am confident that today, just as four years ago, the people want more than promises.

Our vision for the future contains more than promises.

This is our answer to those who, silent about their own plans, ask us to state our objectives.

Of course we will continue to seek to improve working conditions for the workers of America—to reduce hours over-long, to increase wages that spell starvation, to end the labor of children, to wipe out sweatshops. Of course we will continue every effort to end monopoly in business, to support collective bargaining, to stop unfair competition, to abolish dishonorable trade practices. For all these we have only just begun to fight.

Of course we will continue to work for cheaper electricity in the homes and on the farms of America, for better and cheaper transportation, for low interest rates, for sounder home financing, for better banking, for the regulation of security issues, for reciprocal trade among nations, for the wiping out of slums. For all these we have only just begun to fight.

Of course we will continue our efforts in behalf of the farmers of America. With their continued cooperation we will do all in our power to end the piling up of huge surpluses which spelled ruinous prices for their crops. We will persist in successful action for better land use, for reforestation, for the conservation of water all the way from its source to the sea, for drought and flood control, for better marketing facilities for farm commodities, for a definite reduction of farm tenancy, for encouragement of farmer cooperatives, for crop insurance and a stable food supply. For all these we have only just begun to fight.

Of course we will provide useful work for the needy unemployed; we prefer useful work to the pauperism of a dole.

Here and now I want to make myself clear about those who disparage their fellow citizens on the relief rolls. They say that those on relief are not merely jobless—that they are worthless. Their solution for the relief problem is to end relief—to purge the rolls by starvation. To use the language of the stock broker, our needy unemployed would be cared for when, as, and if some fairy godmother should happen on the scene.

You and I will continue to refuse to accept that estimate of our unemployed fellow Americans. Your Government is still on the same side of the street with the Good Samaritan and not with those who pass by on the other side.

Again—what of our objectives?

Of course we will continue our efforts for young men and women so that they may obtain an education and an opportunity to put it to use. Of course we will continue our help for the crippled, for the blind, for the mothers, our insurance for the unemployed, our security for the aged. Of course we will continue to protect the consumer against unnecessary price spreads, against the costs that are added by monopoly and speculation. We will continue our successful efforts to increase his purchasing power and to keep it constant.

For these things, too, and for a multitude of others like them, we have only just begun to fight.

All this—all these objectives—spell peace at home. All our actions, all our ideals, spell also peace with other nations.

Today there is war and rumor of war. We want none of it. But while we guard our shores against threats of war, we will continue to remove the causes of unrest and antagonism at home which might make our people easier victims to those for whom foreign war is profitable. You know well that those who stand to profit by war are not on our side in this campaign.

"Peace on earth, good will toward men"—democracy must cling to that message. For it is my deep conviction that democracy cannot live without that true religion which gives a nation a sense of justice and of moral purpose. Above our political forums, above our market places stand the altars of our faith—altars on which burn the fires of devotion that maintain all that is best in us and all that is best in our Nation.

We have need of that devotion today. It is that which makes it possible for government to persuade those who are mentally prepared to fight each other to go on instead, to work for and to sacrifice for each other. That is why we need to say with the Prophet: "What doth the Lord require of thee—but to do justly, to love mercy and to walk humbly with thy God." That is why the recovery we seek, the recovery we are winning, is more than economic. In it are included justice and love and humility, not for ourselves as individuals alone, but for our Nation.

That is the road to peace.

1. According to Roosevelt, what was the main issue in the election of 1932?

    A. continuance of the presidency
    B. preservation of victories
    C. continuation of policies
    D. restoration of democracy

2. Roosevelt declines to explain the details of his administration's programs because

    A. average Americans couldn't understand them.
    B. spies and opponents would exploit the information.
    C. the programs are changing too quickly.
    D. the programs' records speak for themselves.

3. Which event was bringing Americans suffering in the early 1930s?

    A. World War I
    B. World War II
    C. The Great Depression
    D. The McCarthy Hearings

4. Roosevelt says that he is leading an army primarily composed of

    A. soldiers and sailors who want peace.
    B. elderly pensioners who want benefits.
    C. Americans who want change.
    D. workers who want jobs.

5. Roosevelt refers to the government prior to his administration as all of the following **except**

    A. do-nothings.
    B. war criminals.
    C. a mirage.
    D. a golden calf.

6. Employers try to dissuade workers from voting for Roosevelt primarily by

    A. lying to them about Roosevelt's policies.
    B. threatening to close factories if Roosevelt wins.
    C. refusing to allow Roosevelt supporters to vote.
    D. bribing them to vote for Roosevelt's opponents.

7. According to the document, Roosevelt's opponents would try to end the relief problem through

    A. higher taxes.
    B. starvation.
    C. foreign loans.
    D. deceit.

8. Which of the following should be the central message for democracy?

    A. A penny saved is a penny earned.
    B. Do unto others as you would have them do.
    C. An eye for an eye, a tooth for a tooth.
    D. Peace on earth, good will toward men.

9. What do you think President Roosevelt means when he talks about the "pass-key to the White House"? Do you think this message was phrased well for his audience?

_____

_____

_____

_____

_____

_____

_____

_____

_____

_____

_____

_____

_____

_____

_____

PRESIDENT FRANKLIN ROOSEVELT'S ANNUAL MESSAGE (FOUR FREEDOMS) TO CONGRESS (1941)

Very early in his political career, as state senator and later as governor of New York, President Roosevelt was concerned with human rights in the broadest sense. During 1940, stimulated by a press conference in which he discussed long-range peace objectives, he started collecting ideas for a speech about various rights and freedoms. In his Annual Message to Congress of January 6, 1941, he asked the people to work hard to produce armaments for the democracies of Europe, to pay higher taxes, and to make other sacrifices. Also, in memorable phrases, he envisioned a better future, founded upon four freedoms: the "four essential human freedoms," some traditional and some new ones. The four freedoms he outlined were freedom of speech, freedom of worship, freedom from want, and freedom from fear. As America became engaged in World War II, painter Norman Rockwell did a series of pieces illustrating the four freedoms as international war goals that went beyond just defeating the Axis powers. The paintings went on a nationwide tour to raise money for the war effort. After the war, the four freedoms appeared again imbedded in the Charter of the United Nations.

Mr. President, Mr. Speaker, Members of the Seventy-seventh Congress:

I address you, the Members of the Seventy-seventh Congress, at a moment unprecedented in the history of the Union. I use the word "unprecedented," because at no previous time has American security been as seriously threatened from without as it is today.

Since the permanent formation of our Government under the Constitution, in 1789, most of the periods of crisis in our history have related to our domestic affairs. Fortunately, only one of these— the four-year War Between the States—ever threatened our national unity. Today, thank God, one hundred and thirty million Americans, in forty-eight States, have forgotten points of the compass in our national unity.

It is true that prior to 1914 the United States often had been disturbed by events in other Continents. We had even engaged in two wars with European nations and in a number of undeclared wars in the West Indies, in the Mediterranean and in the Pacific for the maintenance of American rights and for the principles of peaceful commerce. But in no case had a serious threat been raised against our national safety or our continued independence.

What I seek to convey is the historic truth that the United States as a nation has at all times maintained clear, definite opposition, to any attempt to lock us in behind an ancient Chinese wall while the procession of civilization went past. Today, thinking of our children and of their children, we oppose enforced isolation for ourselves or for any other part of the Americas.

That determination of ours, extending over all these years, was proved, for example, during the quarter century of wars following the French Revolution.

While the Napoleonic struggles did threaten interests of the United States because of the French foothold in the West Indies and in Louisiana, and while we engaged in the War of 1812 to vindicate our right to peaceful trade, it is nevertheless clear that neither France nor Great Britain, nor any other nation, was aiming at domination of the whole world.

In like fashion from 1815 to 1914—ninety-nine years—no single war in Europe or in Asia constituted a real threat against our future or against the future of any other American nation.

Except in the Maximilian interlude in Mexico, no foreign power sought to establish itself in this Hemisphere; and the strength of the British fleet in the Atlantic has been a friendly strength. It is still a friendly strength.

Even when the World War broke out in 1914, it seemed to contain only small threat of danger to our own American future. But, as time went on, the American people began to visualize what the downfall of democratic nations might mean to our own democracy.

We need not overemphasize imperfections in the Peace of Versailles. We need not harp on failure of the democracies to deal with problems of world reconstruction. We should remember that the Peace of 1919 was far less unjust than the kind of "pacification" which began even before Munich, and which is being carried on under the new order of tyranny that seeks to spread over every continent today. The American people have unalterably set their faces against that tyranny.

Every realist knows that the democratic way of life is at this moment being directly assailed in every part of the world—assailed either by arms, or by secret spreading of poisonous propaganda by those who seek to destroy unity and promote discord in nations that are still at peace.

During sixteen long months this assault has blotted out the whole pattern of democratic life in an appalling number of independent nations, great and small. The assailants are still on the march, threatening other nations, great and small.

Therefore, as your President, performing my constitutional duty to "give to the Congress information of the state of the Union," I find it, unhappily, necessary to report that the future and the safety of our country and of our democracy are overwhelmingly involved in events far beyond our borders.

Armed defense of democratic existence is now being gallantly waged in four continents. If that defense fails, all the population and all the resources of Europe, Asia, Africa and Australasia will be dominated by the conquerors. Let us remember that the total of those populations and their resources in those four continents greatly exceeds the sum total of the population and the resources of the whole of the Western Hemisphere—many times over.

In times like these it is immature—and incidentally, untrue—for anybody to brag that an unprepared America, single-handed, and with one hand tied behind its back, can hold off the whole world.

No realistic American can expect from a dictator's peace international generosity, or return of true independence, or world disarmament, or freedom of expression, or freedom of religion—or even good business.

Such a peace would bring no security for us or for our neighbors. "Those, who would give up essential liberty to purchase a little temporary safety, deserve neither liberty nor safety."

As a nation, we may take pride in the fact that we are softhearted; but we cannot afford to be soft-headed.

We must always be wary of those who with sounding brass and a tinkling cymbal preach the "ism" of appeasement.

We must especially beware of that small group of selfish men who would clip the wings of the American eagle in order to feather their own nests.

I have recently pointed out how quickly the tempo of modern warfare could bring into our very midst the physical attack which we must eventually expect if the dictator nations win this war.

There is much loose talk of our immunity from immediate and direct invasion from across the seas. Obviously, as long as the British Navy retains its power, no such danger exists. Even if there were no British Navy, it is not probable that any enemy would be stupid enough to attack us by landing troops in the United States from across thousands of miles of ocean, until it had acquired strategic bases from which to operate.

But we learn much from the lessons of the past years in Europe—particularly the lesson of Norway, whose essential seaports were captured by treachery and surprise built up over a series of years.

The first phase of the invasion of this Hemisphere would not be the landing of regular troops. The necessary strategic points would be occupied by secret agents and their dupes—and great numbers of them are already here, and in Latin America.

As long as the aggressor nations maintain the offensive, they—not we—will choose the time and the place and the method of their attack.

That is why the future of all the American Republics is today in serious danger.

That is why this Annual Message to the Congress is unique in our history.

That is why every member of the Executive Branch of the Government and every member of the Congress faces great responsibility and great accountability.

The need of the moment is that our actions and our policy should be devoted primarily—almost exclusively—to meeting this foreign peril. For all our domestic problems are now a part of the great emergency.

Just as our national policy in internal affairs has been based upon a decent respect for the rights and the dignity of all our fellow men within our gates, so our national policy in foreign affairs has been based on a decent respect for the rights and dignity of all nations, large and small. And the justice of morality must and will win in the end.

Our national policy is this:

First, by an impressive expression of the public will and without regard to partisanship, we are committed to all-inclusive national defense.

Second, by an impressive expression of the public will and without regard to partisanship, we are committed to full support of all those resolute peoples, everywhere, who are resisting aggression and are thereby keeping war away from our Hemisphere. By this support, we express our determination that the democratic cause shall prevail; and we strengthen the defense and the security of our own nation.

Third, by an impressive expression of the public will and without regard to partisanship, we are committed to the proposition that principles of morality and considerations for our own security will never permit us to acquiesce in a peace dictated by aggressors and sponsored by appeasers. We know that enduring peace cannot be bought at the cost of other people's freedom.

In the recent national election there was no substantial difference between the two great parties in respect to that national policy. No issue was fought out on this line before the American electorate. Today it is abundantly evident that American citizens everywhere are demanding and supporting speedy and complete action in recognition of obvious danger.

Therefore, the immediate need is a swift and driving increase in our armament production.

Leaders of industry and labor have responded to our summons. Goals of speed have been set. In some cases these goals are being reached ahead of time; in some cases we are on schedule; in other cases there are slight but not serious delays; and in some cases—and I am sorry to say very important cases—we are all concerned by the slowness of the accomplishment of our plans.

The Army and Navy, however, have made substantial progress during the past year. Actual experience is improving and speeding up our methods of production with every passing day. And today's best is not good enough for tomorrow.

I am not satisfied with the progress thus far made. The men in charge of the program represent the best in training, in ability, and in patriotism. They are not satisfied with the progress thus far made. None of us will be satisfied until the job is done.

No matter whether the original goal was set too high or too low, our objective is quicker and better results. To give you two illustrations:

We are behind schedule in turning out finished airplanes; we are working day and night to solve the innumerable problems and to catch up.

We are ahead of schedule in building warships but we are working to get even further ahead of that schedule.

To change a whole nation from a basis of peacetime production of implements of peace to a basis of wartime production of implements of war is no small task. And the greatest difficulty comes at the beginning of the program, when new tools, new plant facilities, new assembly lines, and new ship ways must first be constructed before the actual materiel begins to flow steadily and speedily from them.

The Congress, of course, must rightly keep itself informed at all times of the progress of the program. However, there is certain information, as the Congress itself will readily recognize, which, in the interests of our own security and those of the nations that we are supporting, must of needs be kept in confidence.

New circumstances are constantly begetting new needs for our safety. I shall ask this Congress for greatly increased new appropriations and authorizations to carry on what we have begun.

I also ask this Congress for authority and for funds sufficient to manufacture additional munitions and war supplies of many kinds, to be turned over to those nations which are now in actual war with aggressor nations.

Our most useful and immediate role is to act as an arsenal for them as well as for ourselves. They do not need man power, but they do need billions of dollars worth of the weapons of defense.

The time is near when they will not be able to pay for them all in ready cash. We cannot, and we will not, tell them that they must surrender, merely because of present inability to pay for the weapons which we know they must have.

I do not recommend that we make them a loan of dollars with which to pay for these weapons—a loan to be repaid in dollars.

I recommend that we make it possible for those nations to continue to obtain war materials in the United States, fitting their orders into our own program. Nearly all their materiel would, if the time ever came, be useful for our own defense.

Taking counsel of expert military and naval authorities, considering what is best for our own security, we are free to decide how much should be kept here and how much should be sent abroad to our friends who by their determined and heroic resistance are giving us time in which to make ready our own defense.

For what we send abroad, we shall be repaid within a reasonable time following the close of hostilities, in similar materials, or, at our option, in other goods of many kinds, which they can produce and which we need.

Let us say to the democracies: "We Americans are vitally concerned in your defense of freedom. We are putting forth our energies, our resources and our organizing powers to give you the strength to regain and maintain a free world. We shall send you, in ever-increasing numbers, ships, planes, tanks, guns. This is our purpose and our pledge."

In fulfillment of this purpose we will not be intimidated by the threats of dictators that they will regard as a breach of international law or as an act of war our aid to the democracies which dare to resist their aggression. Such aid is not an act of war, even if a dictator should unilaterally proclaim it so to be.

When the dictators, if the dictators, are ready to make war upon us, they will not wait for an act of war on our part. They did not wait for Norway or Belgium or the Netherlands to commit an act of war.

Their only interest is in a new one-way international law, which lacks mutuality in its observance, and, therefore, becomes an instrument of oppression.

The happiness of future generations of Americans may well depend upon how effective and how immediate we can make our aid felt. No one can tell the exact character of the emergency situations that we may be called upon to meet. The Nation's hands must not be tied when the Nation's life is in danger.

We must all prepare to make the sacrifices that the emergency—almost as serious as war itself—demands. Whatever stands in the way of speed and efficiency in defense preparations must give way to the national need.

A free nation has the right to expect full cooperation from all groups. A free nation has the right to look to the leaders of business, of labor, and of agriculture to take the lead in stimulating effort, not among other groups but within their own groups.

The best way of dealing with the few slackers or trouble makers in our midst is, first, to shame them by patriotic example, and, if that fails, to use the sovereignty of Government to save Government.

As men do not live by bread alone, they do not fight by armaments alone. Those who man our defenses, and those behind them who build our defenses, must have the stamina and the courage which come from unshakable belief in the manner of life which they are defending. The mighty action that we are calling for cannot be based on a disregard of all things worth fighting for.

The Nation takes great satisfaction and much strength from the things which have been done to make its people conscious of their individual stake in the preservation of democratic life in America. Those things have toughened the fibre of our people, have renewed their faith and strengthened their devotion to the institutions we make ready to protect.

Certainly this is no time for any of us to stop thinking about the social and economic problems which are the root cause of the social revolution which is today a supreme factor in the world.

For there is nothing mysterious about the foundations of a healthy and strong democracy. The basic things expected by our people of their political and economic systems are simple. They are:

Equality of opportunity for youth and for others.

Jobs for those who can work.

Security for those who need it.

The ending of special privilege for the few.

The preservation of civil liberties for all.

The enjoyment of the fruits of scientific progress in a wider and constantly rising standard of living.

These are the simple, basic things that must never be lost sight of in the turmoil and unbelievable complexity of our modern world. The inner and abiding strength of our economic and political systems is dependent upon the degree to which they fulfill these expectations.

Many subjects connected with our social economy call for immediate improvement.

As examples:

We should bring more citizens under the coverage of old-age pensions and unemployment insurance.

We should widen the opportunities for adequate medical care.

We should plan a better system by which persons deserving or needing gainful employment may obtain it.

I have called for personal sacrifice. I am assured of the willingness of almost all Americans to respond to that call.

A part of the sacrifice means the payment of more money in taxes. In my Budget Message I shall recommend that a greater portion of this great defense program be paid for from taxation than we are paying today. No person should try, or be allowed, to get rich out of this program; and the principle of tax payments in accordance with ability to pay should be constantly before our eyes to guide our legislation.

If the Congress maintains these principles, the voters, putting patriotism ahead of pocketbooks, will give you their applause.

In the future days, which we seek to make secure, we look forward to a world founded upon four essential human freedoms.

The first is freedom of speech and expression—everywhere in the world.

The second is freedom of every person to worship God in his own way—everywhere in the world.

The third is freedom from want—which, translated into world terms, means economic understandings which will secure to every nation a healthy peacetime life for its inhabitants—everywhere in the world.

The fourth is freedom from fear—which, translated into world terms, means a world-wide reduction of armaments to such a point and in such a thorough fashion that no nation will be in a position to commit an act of physical aggression against any neighbor—anywhere in the world.

That is no vision of a distant millennium. It is a definite basis for a kind of world attainable in our own time and generation. That kind of world is the very antithesis of the so-called new order of tyranny which the dictators seek to create with the crash of a bomb.

To that new order we oppose the greater conception—the moral order. A good society is able to face schemes of world domination and foreign revolutions alike without fear.

Since the beginning of our American history, we have been engaged in change—in a perpetual peaceful revolution—a revolution which goes on steadily, quietly adjusting itself to changing conditions—without the concentration camp or the quick-lime in the ditch. The world order which we seek is the cooperation of free countries, working together in a friendly, civilized society.

This nation has placed its destiny in the hands and heads and hearts of its millions of free men and women; and its faith in freedom under the guidance of God. Freedom means the supremacy of human rights everywhere. Our support goes to those who struggle to gain those rights or keep them. Our strength is our unity of purpose. To that high concept there can be no end save victory.

1. What does President Roosevelt believe about America's attainment of the Four Freedoms?

    A. It occurred when the Constitution was ratified.
    B. It occurred at the end of the Great Depression.
    C. It can occur during the lifetime of his generation.
    D. It will occur sometime in the coming millennium.

2. The main concern Roosevelt is addressing in this document is

    A. The Spanish-American War.
    B. The Mexican Border War.
    C. World War I.
    D. World War II.

3. According to the document, America's **best** safeguard from attack is the

   A. British navy.
   B. American air force.
   C. Russian army.
   D. French resistance.

4. According to Roosevelt, the basis of America's foreign policy is

   A. a strong military presence.
   B. an isolationist attitude.
   C. respect for the rights of other nations.
   D. determination to defeat aggressor nations.

5. What is Roosevelt's reaction to America's current production of war materials?

   A. pride
   B. dissatisfaction
   C. shock
   D. pleasure

6. If the "dictator nations" win the war, America can expect

   A. good business.
   B. uneasy peace.
   C. certain attack.
   D. shaky negotiation.

7. The four freedoms are freedom of speech, freedom from want, freedom from fear, and freedom of

   A. expression.
   B. choice.
   C. liberty.
   D. worship.

8. America's allies in Europe are in greatest need of more

   A. soldiers.
   B. weapons.
   C. encouragement.
   D. money.

9. The development of America can **best** be described as

   A. a thunderous maelstrom.
   B. a march toward uncertain horizons.
   C. a perpetual peaceful revolution.
   D. an endless struggle against oppression.

10. What are President Roosevelt's ideas about a possible attack on America? Do you think his ideas still apply today?

_____

_____

_____

_____

_____

_____

_____

_____

_____

_____

_____

_____

_____

_____

_____

_____

_____

_____

_____

_____

_____

_____

Lend-Lease Act (1941)

In July 1940, after Britain had sustained the loss of eleven destroyers to the German Navy over a ten-day period, newly elected British Prime Minister Winston Churchill requested help from President Roosevelt. Roosevelt responded by exchanging 50 destroyers for 99-year leases on British bases in the Caribbean and Newfoundland. As a result, a major foreign policy debate erupted over whether the United States should aid Great Britain or maintain strict neutrality.

In the 1940 presidential election campaign, Roosevelt promised to keep America out of the war. He stated, "I have said this before, but I shall say it again and again and again; your boys are not going to be sent into any foreign wars." Nevertheless, FDR wanted to support Britain and believed the United States should serve as a "great arsenal of democracy." Churchill pleaded, "Give us the tools and we'll finish the job." In January 1941, following up on his campaign pledge and the prime minister's appeal for arms, Roosevelt proposed to Congress a new military aid bill.

The plan proposed by FDR was to "lend-lease or otherwise dispose of arms" and other supplies needed by any country whose security was vital to the defense of the United States. In support of the bill, Secretary of War Henry L. Stimson told the Senate Foreign Relations Committee during the debate over lend-lease, "We are buying . . . not lending. We are buying our own security while we prepare. By our delay during the past six years, while Germany was preparing, we find ourselves unprepared and unarmed, facing a thoroughly prepared and armed potential enemy." Following two months of debate, Congress passed the Lend-Lease Act, meeting Great Britain's deep need for supplies and allowing the United States to prepare for war while remaining officially neutral.

A BILL

Further to promote the defense of the United States, and for other purposes.

Be it enacted by the Senate add House of Representatives of the United States of America in Congress assembled, That this Act may be cited as "An Act to Promote the Defense of the United States".

SEC. 2. As used in this Act—

(a) The term "defense article" means—

(1) Any weapon, munition, aircraft, vessel, or boat;

(2) Any machinery, facility, tool, material, or supply necessary for the manufacture, production, processing, repair, servicing, or operation of any article described in this subsection;

(3) Any component material or part of or equipment for any article described in this subsection;

(4) Any agricultural, industrial or other commodity or article for defense.

Such term "defense article" includes any article described in this subsection: Manufactured or procured pursuant to section 3, or to which the United States or any foreign government has or hereafter acquires title, possession, or control.

(b) The term "defense information" means any plan, specification, design, prototype, or information pertaining to any defense article.

SEC. 3. (a) Notwithstanding the provisions of any other law, the President may, from time to time. when he deems it in the interest of national defense, authorize the Secretary of War, the Secretary of the Navy, or the bead of any other department or agency of the Government—

(1) To manufacture in arsenals, factories, and shipyards under their jurisdiction, or otherwise procure, to the extent to which funds are made available therefor, or contracts are authorized from time to time by the Congress, or both, any defense article for the government of any country whose defense the President deems vital to the defense of the United States.

(2) To sell, transfer title to, exchange, lease, lend, or otherwise dispose of, to any such government any defense article, but no defense article not manufactured or procured under paragraph (1) shall in any way be disposed of under this paragraph, except after consultation with the Chief of Staff of the Army or the Chief of Naval Operations of the Navy, or both. The value of defense articles disposed of in any way under authority of this paragraph, and procured from funds heretofore appropriated, shall not exceed $1,300,000,000. The value of such defense articles shall be determined by the head of the department or agency concerned or such other department, agency or officer as shall be designated in the manner provided in the rules and regulations issued hereunder. Defense articles procured from funds hereafter appropriated to any department or agency of the Government, other than from funds authorized to he appropriated under this Act shall not be disposed of in any way under authority of this paragraph except to the extent hereafter authorized by the Congress in the Acts appropriating such funds or otherwise.

(3) To test, inspect, prove, repair, outfit, recondition, or otherwise to place in good working order, to the extent to which funds are made available therefor, or contracts are authorized from time to time by the Congress, or both, any defense article for any such government, or to procure any or all such services by private contract.

(4) To communicate to any such government any defense information pertaining to any defense article furnished to such government under paragraph (2) of this subsection.

(5) To release for export any defense article disposed of in any way under this subsection to any such government.

(b) The terms and conditions upon which any such foreign government receives any aid authorized under subsection (a) shall be those which the President deems satisfactory, and the benefit to the United States may he payment or repayment in kind or property, or any other direct or indirect benefit which the President deems satisfactory.

(c) After June 30, 1943, or after the passage of a concurrent resolution by the two Houses before June 30, 1943, which declares that the powers conferred by or pursuant to subsection (a) are no longer necessary to promote the defense of the United States, neither the President nor the head of any department or agency shall exercise any of the powers conferred by or pursuant to subsection (a) except that until July 1, 1946, any of such powers may be exercised to the extent necessary to carry out a contract or agreement with such a foreign government made before July 1, 1943, or before the passage of such concurrent resolution, whichever is the earlier.

(d) Nothing in this Act shall be construed to authorize or to permit the authorization of convoying vessels by naval vessels of the United States.

(e) Nothing in this Act shall be construed to authorize or to permit the authorization of the entry of any American vessel into a combat area in violation of section 3 of the neutrality Act of 1939.

SEC. 4. All contracts or agreements made for the disposition of any defense article or defense information pursuant to section 3 shall contain a clause by which the foreign government undertakes that it will not, without the consent of the President, transfer title to or possession of such defense article or defense information by gift, sale, or otherwise, or permit its use by anyone not an officer, employee, or agent of such foreign government.

SEC. 5. (a) The Secretary of War, the Secretary of the Navy, or the head of any other department or agency of the Government involved shall when any such defense article or defense information is exported, immediately inform the department or agency designated by the President to administer section 6 of the Act of July 2, 1940 (54 Stat. 714). of the quantities, character, value, terms of disposition and destination of the article and information so exported.

(b) The President from time to time, but not less frequently than once every ninety days, shall transmit to the Congress a report of operations under this Act except such information as he deems incompatible with the public interest to disclose. Reports provided for under this subsection shall be transmitted to the Secretary of the Senate or the Clerk of the House of representatives, as the case may be, if the Senate or the House of Representatives, as the case may be, is not in session.

SEC. 6. (a) There is hereby authorized to be appropriated from time to time, out of any money in the Treasury not otherwise appropriated, such amounts as may be necessary to carry out the provisions and accomplish the purposes of this Act.

(b) All money and all property which is converted into money received under section 3 from any government shall, with the approval of the Director of the Budget. revert to the respective appropriation or appropriations out of which funds were expended with respect to the defense article or defense information for which such consideration is received, and shall be available for expenditure for the purpose for which such expended funds were appropriated by law, during the fiscal year in which such funds are received and the ensuing fiscal year; but in no event shall any funds so received be available for expenditure after June 30, 1946.

SEC. 7. The Secretary of War, the Secretary of the Navy, and the head of the department or agency shall in all contracts or agreements for the disposition of any defense article or defense information fully protect the rights of all citizens of the United States who have patent rights in and to any such article or information which is hereby authorized to he disposed of and the payments collected for royalties on such patents shall be paid to the owners and holders of such patents.

SEC. 8. The Secretaries of War and of the Navy are hereby authorized to purchase or otherwise acquire arms, ammunition, and implements of war produced within the jurisdiction of any country to which section 3 is applicable, whenever the President deems such purchase or acquisition to be necessary in the interests of the defense of the United States.

SEC. 9. The President may, from time to time, promulgate such rules and regulations as may be necessary and proper to carry out any of the provisions of this Act; and he may exercise any power or authority conferred on him by this Act through such department, agency, or officer as be shall direct.

SEC. 10. Nothing in this Act shall be construed to change existing law relating to the use of the land and naval forces of the United States, except insofar as such use relates to the manufacture, procurement, and repair of defense articles, the communication of information and other noncombatant purposes enumerated in this Act.

SEC. 11. If any provision of this Act or the application of such provision to any circumstance shall be held invalid, the validity of the remainder of the Act and the applicability of such provision to other circumstances shall not be affected thereby.

Approved, March 11, 1941.

1. As defined by this document, a battleship would be an example of

    A. leased munitions.
    B. a leased armament.
    C. a defense article.
    D. defense information.

2. All of the following are examples of "defense information" **except**

    A. knowledge of an enemy's secrets.
    B. designs for a new missile.
    C. the specifications of a fortress.
    D. the blueprints of a military aircraft.

3. The president must report operations under this act to the

    A. Allied nations.
    B. American public.
    C. Congress.
    D. Supreme Court.

4. The Lend-Lease Act allows for all of the following **except**

    A. manufacturing arsenals, factories, and shipyards.
    B. giving defense information to participating governments.
    C. appropriating additional money from the Treasury.
    D. sending American vessels into combat areas.

5. Who decides the recipient of the items covered by this act?

    A. the president
    B. Congress
    C. Secretary of War
    D. Chief of Staff of the army or Chief of Naval Operations of the navy

6. Do you think that the name designated for the act is accurate or is it misleading propaganda? Support your response.

_____

_____

_____

_____

_____

_____

_____

_____

_____

_____

_____

_____

_____

_____

_____

_____

_____

_____

_____

_____

_____

_____

74

EXECUTIVE ORDER 8802: PROHIBITION OF DISCRIMINATION IN THE DEFENSE INDUSTRY (1941)

In early July 1941, millions of jobs were being created, primarily in urban areas, as the United States prepared for war. When large numbers of African Americans moved to cities in the north and west to work in defense industries, they were often met with violence and discrimination. In response, A. Philip Randolph, president of the Brotherhood of Sleeping Car Porters, and other black leaders met with Eleanor Roosevelt and members of the president's cabinet. Randolph presented a list of grievances regarding the civil rights of African Americans, demanding that an executive order be issued to stop job discrimination in the defense industry. Randolph and the others threatened that they were prepared to bring "ten, twenty, fifty thousand Negroes on the White House lawn" if their demands were not met. After consultation with his advisers, Roosevelt responded to the black leaders and issued Executive Order 8802, which declared, "There shall be no discrimination in the employment of workers in defense industries and in Government, because of race, creed, color, or national origin." It was the first presidential directive on race since Reconstruction. The order also established the Fair Employment Practices Committee to investigate incidents of discrimination.

Reaffirming Policy Of Full Participation In The Defense Program By All Persons, Regardless Of Race, Creed, Color, Or National Origin, And Directing Certain Action In Furtherance Of Said Policy

June 25, 1941

WHEREAS it is the policy of the United States to encourage full participation in the national defense program by all citizens of the United States, regardless of race, creed, color, or national origin, in the firm belief that the democratic way of life within the Nation can be defended successfully only with the help and support of all groups within its borders; and

WHEREAS there is evidence that available and needed workers have been barred from employment in industries engaged in defense production solely because of considerations of race, creed, color, or national origin, to the detriment of workers' morale and of national unity:

NOW, THEREFORE, by virtue of the authority vested in me by the Constitution and the statutes, and as a prerequisite to the successful conduct of our national defense production effort, I do hereby reaffirm the policy of the United States that there shall be no discrimination in the employment of workers in defense industries or government because of race, creed, color, or national origin, and I do hereby declare that it is the duty of employers and of labor organizations, in furtherance of said policy and of this order, to provide for the full and equitable participation of all workers in defense industries, without discrimination because of race, creed, color, or national origin;

And it is hereby ordered as follows:

1. All departments and agencies of the Government of the United States concerned with vocational and training programs for defense production shall take special measures appropriate to assure that such programs are administered without discrimination because of race, creed, color, or national origin;

2. All contracting agencies of the Government of the United States shall include in all defense contracts hereafter negotiated by them a provision obligating the contractor not to discriminate against any worker because of race, creed, color, or national origin;

3. There is established in the Office of Production Management a Committee on Fair Employment Practice, which shall consist of a chairman and four other members to be appointed by the President. The Chairman and members of the Committee shall serve as such without compensation but shall be entitled to actual and necessary transportation, subsistence and other expenses incidental to performance of their duties. The Committee shall receive and investigate complaints of discrimination in violation of the provisions of this order and shall take appropriate steps to redress grievances which it finds to be valid. The Committee shall also recommend to the several departments and agencies of the Government of the United States and to the President all measures which may be deemed by it necessary or proper to effectuate the provisions of this order.

Franklin D. Roosevelt

The White House,

June 25, 1941

1. The Committee on Fair Employment Practice was formed in order to

   A. receive, investigate, and redress grievances.
   B. circulate news of the executive order.
   C. inspect government munitions factories.
   D. meet with civil and workers' rights leaders.

2. Workers in the defense industry can only legally be judged according to their

   A. creed.
   B. skills.
   C. color.
   D. national origin.

3. This executive order was aimed primarily at

   A. minorities.
   B. government officials.
   C. army officers.
   D. employers.

4. Discrimination against defense workers in America was harmful for all of the following reasons **except** that it

   A. kept workers from helping the defense effort.
   B. encouraged other countries to discriminate.
   C. harmed workers' morale nationwide.
   D. strained the concept of national unity.

5. The orders put forth in this document extend to

    A. the American military.
    B. workers in other countries.
    C. most civilian enterprises.
    D. worker training programs.

5. For whom do you think Roosevelt wrote this document? Use details and information from the document to support your answer.

_____

_____

_____

_____

_____

_____

_____

_____

_____

_____

_____

_____

_____

_____

_____

_____

_____

_____

_____

_____

Joint Address to Congress Leading to a Declaration of War Against Japan (1941)

On December 7, 1941, the U.S. naval base on the island of Oahu, Hawaii, was subject to an attack that was one of the greatest military surprises in the history of warfare. In less than two hours, the U.S. Pacific Fleet was devastated. More than 3,500 Americans were killed or wounded. The Japanese attack on Pearl Harbor catapulted the United States into World War II.

The American people were outraged. Though diplomatic relations between the United States and Japan were deteriorating, they had not yet broken off at the time of the attack. Instantly, the incident united the American people in a massive mobilization for war and strengthened American resolve to guard against any future lapse of military alertness.

Early on the afternoon of December 7, 1941, President Franklin D. Roosevelt and his chief foreign policy aide, Harry Hopkins, were interrupted by a telephone call from Secretary of War Henry Stimson and told that the Japanese had attacked Pearl Harbor. At about 5 p.m.—following meetings with his military advisers—the president calmly and decisively dictated to his secretary, Grace Tully, a request to Congress for a declaration of war. He had composed the speech in his head after deciding on a brief, uncomplicated appeal to the people of the United States, rather than a thorough recitation of Japanese treachery, as Secretary of State Cordell Hull had urged.

President Roosevelt then revised the typed draft—marking it up, updating military information, and selecting alternative wording that strengthened the tone of the speech. He made the most significant change in the critical first line, which originally read, "a date which will live in world history." Grace Tully then prepared the final reading copy, which Roosevelt subsequently altered in three more places.

On December 8th at 12:30 p.m., Roosevelt addressed a joint session of Congress and, via radio, the nation. The Senate responded with a unanimous vote in support of war; only Montana pacifist Jeanette Rankin dissented in the House. At 4 p.m. that same afternoon, President Roosevelt signed the declaration of war.

Mr. Vice President, and Mr. Speaker, and Members of the Senate and House of Representatives:

Yesterday, December 7, 1941—a date which will live in infamy—the United States of America was suddenly and deliberately attacked by naval and air forces of the Empire of Japan.

The United States was at peace with that Nation and, at the solicitation of Japan, was still in conversation with its Government and its Emperor looking toward the maintenance of peace in the Pacific. Indeed, one hour after Japanese air squadrons had commenced bombing in the American Island of Oahu, the Japanese Ambassador to the United States and his colleague delivered to our Secretary of State a formal reply to a recent American message. And while this reply stated that it seemed useless to continue the existing diplomatic negotiations, it contained no threat or hint of war or of armed attack.

It will be recorded that the distance of Hawaii from Japan makes it obvious that the attack was deliberately planned many days or even weeks ago. During the intervening time the Japanese

Government has deliberately sought to deceive the United States by false statements and expressions of hope for continued peace.

The attack yesterday on the Hawaiian Islands has caused severe damage to American naval and military forces. I regret to tell you that very many American lives have been lost. In addition American ships have been reported torpedoed on the high seas between San Francisco and Honolulu.

Yesterday the Japanese Government also launched an attack against Malaya.

Last night Japanese forces attacked Hong Kong.

Last night Japanese forces attacked Guam.

Last night Japanese forces attacked the Philippine Islands.

Last night the Japanese attacked Wake Island. And this morning the Japanese attacked Midway Island.

Japan has, therefore, undertaken a surprise offensive extending throughout the Pacific area. The facts of yesterday and today speak for themselves. The people of the United States have already formed their opinions and well understand the implications to the very life and safety of our Nation.

As Commander in Chief of the Army and Navy I have directed that all measures be taken for our defense.

But always will our whole Nation remember the character of the onslaught against us.

No matter how long it may take us to overcome this premeditated invasion, the American people in their righteous might will win through to absolute victory. I believe that I interpret the will of the Congress and of the people when I assert that we will not only defend ourselves to the uttermost but will make it very certain that this form of treachery shall never again endanger us.

Hostilities exist. There is no blinking at the fact that our people, our territory, and our interests are in grave danger.

With confidence in our armed forces—with the unbounding determination of our people—we will gain the inevitable triumph—so help us God.

I ask that the Congress declare that since the unprovoked and dastardly attack by Japan on Sunday, December 7, 1941, a state of war has existed between the United States and the Japanese Empire.

1. The Japanese Attack on Pearl Harbor was all of the following **except**

    A. deliberate.
    B. premeditated.
    C. expected.
    D. sudden.

2. According to the document, the United States believed that the attack on Pearl Harbor was planned days or weeks in advance because of the

    A. deteriorating relations with Japan.
    B. distance between Hawaii and Japan.
    C. number of troops deployed in Hawaii.
    D. types of weapons used against Americans.

3. Which of the following was **not** attacked by Japan?

    A. Guam
    B. Wake Island
    C. Midway Island
    D. San Francisco

4. How do you think President Roosevelt felt about declaring war against Japan? Use details from the document to support your answer.

_____

_____

_____

_____

_____

_____

_____

_____

_____

_____

_____

_____

_____

_____

_____

_____

_____

_____

5. President Roosevelt said, "our nation will always remember the character of the onslaught against us." Do you think this is true? Why or why not?

_____

_____

_____

_____

_____

_____

_____

_____

_____

_____

_____

_____

_____

_____

_____

_____

_____

_____

_____

_____

_____

_____

_____

EXECUTIVE ORDER 9066:
JAPANESE RELOCATION ORDER (1942)

Between 1861 and 1940, approximately 275,000 Japanese immigrated to Hawaii and the mainland United States, the majority arriving between 1898 and 1924, when quotas were adopted that ended Asian immigration. Many worked in Hawaiian sugarcane fields as contract laborers. After their contracts expired, a small number remained and opened up shops. Other Japanese immigrants settled on the west coast of mainland United States, cultivating marginal farmlands and fruit orchards, fishing, and operating small businesses. Their efforts yielded impressive results. Japanese Americans controled less than four percent of California's farmland in 1940, but they produced more than ten percent of the total value of the state's farm resources.

As was the case with other immigrant groups, Japanese Americans settled in ethnic neighborhoods and established their own schools, houses of worship, and economic and cultural institutions. Ethnic concentration was further increased by real estate agents who would not sell properties to Japanese Americans outside of existing Japanese enclaves. Furthermore, a 1913 act passed by the California Assembly restricting land ownership to those eligible to be citizens. In 1922, the U.S. Supreme Court, in Ozawa v. United States, *upheld the government's right to deny U.S. citizenship to Japanese immigrants.*

Envy over economic success combined with distrust over cultural separateness and longstanding anti-Asian racism turned into disaster when the Empire of Japan attacked Pearl Harbor on December 7, 1941. Lobbyists from western states, many representing competing economic interests or nativist groups, pressured Congress and the president to remove persons of Japanese descent from the west coast, both foreign-born (issei—meaning "first generation" of Japanese in the U.S.) and American citizens (nisei—the second generation of Japanese in America, U.S. citizens by birthright). During congressional committee hearings, Department of Justice representatives raised constitutional and ethical objections to the proposal, so the U.S. Army carried out the task instead. The west coast was divided into military zones. On February 19, 1942, President Franklin D. Roosevelt issued Executive Order 9066, which authorized exclusion. Congress then implemented the order on March 21, 1942, by passing Public Law 503.

After encouraging voluntary evacuation of the areas, the Western Defense Command began involuntary removal and detention of west coast residents of Japanese ancestry. In the next six months, approximately 122,000 men, women, and children were moved to assembly centers. They were then evacuated to and confined in isolated, fenced, and guarded relocation centers, known as "internment camps." The ten relocation sites were in remote areas in six western states and Arkansas: Heart Mountain in Wyoming, Tule Lake and Manzanar in California, Topaz in Utah, Poston and Gila River in Arizona, Granada in Colorado, Minidoka in Idaho, and Jerome and Rowher in Arkansas.

Nearly 70,000 of the evacuees were American citizens. The government made no charges against them, nor could they appeal their incarceration. All lost personal liberties; most lost homes and property as well. Although several Japanese Americans challenged the government's actions in court cases, the Supreme Court upheld their legality. Nisei were nevertheless encouraged to serve in the armed forces and some were also drafted. All together, more than 30,000 Japanese Americans served with distinction during World War II in segregated units.

82

For many years after the war, various individuals and groups sought compensation for the internees. The speed of the evacuation forced many homeowners and businessmen to sell out quickly; total property loss is estimated at $1.3 billion and net income loss at $2.7 billion (calculated in 1983 dollars). The Japanese American Evacuation Claims Act of 1948, with amendments in 1951 and 1965, provided token payments for some property losses. More serious efforts to make amends took place in the early 1980s, when the congressionally established Commission on Wartime Relocation and the Internment of Civilians held investigations and made recommendations. As a result, several bills were introduced in Congress from 1984 until 1988, when Public Law 100-383 — which acknowledged the injustice of the internment, apologized for it, and provided for restitution — was passed.

The President

Executive Order

Authorizing the Secretary of War to Prescribe Military Areas

Whereas the successful prosecution of the war requires every possible protection against espionage and against sabotage to national-defense material, national-defense premises, and national-defense utilities . . .

Now, therefore, by virtue of the authority vested in me as President of the United States, and Commander in Chief of the Army and Navy, I hereby authorize and direct the Secretary of War, and the Military Commanders whom he may from time to time designate, whenever he or any designated Commander deems such action necessary or desirable, to prescribe military areas in such places and of such extent as he or the appropriate Military Commander may determine, from which any or all persons may be excluded, and with respect to which, the right of any person to enter, remain in, or leave shall be subject to whatever restrictions the Secretary of War or the appropriate Military Commander may impose in his discretion. The Secretary of War is hereby authorized to provide for residents of any such area who are excluded therefrom, such transportation, food, shelter, and other accommodations as may be necessary, in the judgment of the Secretary of War or the said Military Commander, and until other arrangements are made, to accomplish the purpose of this order. The designation of military areas in any region or locality shall supersede designations of prohibited and restricted areas by the Attorney General under the Proclamations of December 7 and 8, 1941, and shall supersede the responsibility and authority of the Attorney General under the said Proclamations in respect of such prohibited and restricted areas.

I hereby further authorize and direct the Secretary of War and the said Military Commanders to take such other steps as he or the appropriate Military Commander may deem advisable to enforce compliance with the restrictions applicable to each Military area hereinabove authorized to be designated, including the use of Federal troops and other Federal Agencies, with authority to accept assistance of state and local agencies.

I hereby further authorize and direct all Executive Departments, independent establishments and other Federal Agencies, to assist the Secretary of War or the said Military Commanders in carrying out this Executive Order, including the furnishing of medical aid, hospitalization, food, clothing, transportation, use of land, shelter, and other supplies, equipment, utilities, facilities, and services. This order shall not be construed as modifying or limiting in any way the authority heretofore granted under Executive Order No. 8972, dated December 12, 1941, nor shall it be construed as limiting or modifying the duty and responsibility of the Federal Bureau of Investigation, with respect to the investigation of alleged acts of sabotage or the duty and responsibility of the Attorney General and the Department of Justice under the Proclamations of December 7 and 8, 1941, prescribing regulations for the conduct and control of alien enemies, except as such duty and responsibility is superseded by the designation of military areas hereunder.

Franklin D. Roosevelt

The White House,

February 19, 1942

1. Most of this document discusses

   A. how military commanders are chosen.
   B. the duties of federal agencies.
   C. the responsibilities of the Secretary of War.
   D. how federal troops will be utilized.

2. Which of the following is **not** mentioned as something to be furnished by federal agencies?

   A. weapons
   B. medical aid
   C. transportation
   D. shelter

3. According to the document, who is responsible for the investigation of alleged acts of sabotage?

   A. Commander in Chief
   B. Attorney General
   C. Secretary of War
   D. Federal Bureau of Investigation

4. Why did the president want to establish military areas? Use details and information of the document to support your answer.

_____

_____

_____

_____

_____

_____

_____

_____

_____

_____

_____

_____

_____

_____

_____

_____

_____

_____

5. Do you think that the relocation of the Japanese was necessary and appropriate? Why or why not?

_____

_____

_____

_____

_____

_____

_____

_____

_____

_____

_____

_____

_____

_____

_____

KOREMATSU V. UNITED STATES (1944)

Prejudice against immigrants from Asia had been longstanding on the west coast when World War II broke out following the Japanese attack on Pearl Harbor. Within a few weeks, the demand spread that Japanese Americans—both naturalized citizens as well as those born in the United States, any of whom might be "saboteurs" or "spies"—be removed from the west coast before the Japanese invaded. The fact that no proof existed that a single one of these people constituted a threat to the United States made no difference. Even the respected columnist Walter Lippmann informed his readers that "nobody's constitutional rights include the right to reside and do business on a battlefield. There is plenty of room elsewhere for him to exercise his rights."

On February 19, 1942, President Roosevelt signed Executive Order 9066 authorizing the Secretary of War to designate parts of the country as "military areas" from which any and all persons might be excluded, and in which travel restrictions might be imposed. A few weeks later, General John L. DeWitt, in charge of the Western Defense Command, designated the entire Pacific coast as a military area because of its susceptibility to attack. Curfews were established. Japanese Americans were at first prohibited from leaving the area and then from being in the area. The only way Japanese Americans could comply with these contradictory orders was to submit to evacuation to relocation centers in the interior.

The relocation program—through which 110,000 men, women and children were sent to what were in essence prison camps—constituted the most serious invasion of individual rights by the federal government in the nation's history. The entire operation proceeded on the racist assumption that anyone of Japanese ancestry was a traitor.

In wartime, the old saying goes, law is silent; the Supreme Court, which had only recently begun to play a stronger role in protecting minority rights, was loath to interfere with what the administration considered a necessary war measure. Three cases testing the constitutionality of the evacuation orders were heard by the court. In the first case, Hirabayashi v. United States *(1943), the court sustained the legitimacy of the curfew, but evaded ruling on the wider implications of relocation.*

In the second case, Korematsu v. United States, *the court could no longer ignore the core issue of whether loyal citizens could be summarily relocated to detention camps solely on the basis of their race. Although a majority of the court agreed with Justice Black's view that military necessity justified the relocation, three members of the court—Frank Murphy, Owen J. Roberts and Robert H. Jackson—dissented. Justice Murphy's dissent, which most bluntly dealt with what he termed a "legalization of racism," is included here.*

On the same day, the Supreme Court unanimously authorized a writit of habeas corpus *for Mitsuye Endo, a citizen whose loyalty had been clearly established. The court's rulings in* Hirabayashi *and* Korematsu *were criticized by many civil libertarians and scholars from the start. There has been a general condemnation of them ever since.*

After the war ended, the internment haunted the nation's conscience as well. In 1948, Congress took the first step in making amends, enacting the Japanese American Evacuation Claims Act to provide some monetary compensation to those who had lost homes and businesses because of the order. In 1980, Congress again opened the internment issue, and this time a stream of witnesses testified,

86

many of them for the first time, of the hardships and psychological trauma they had suffered. The resulting report, Personal Justice Denied *(1983), condemned the removal as unjustified by military necessity, and also concluded that the Supreme Court decisions had been "overruled in the court of history."*

Justice Black delivered the opinion of the Court.

It should be noted, to begin with, that all legal restrictions which curtail the civil rights of a single racial group are immediately suspect. That is not to say that all such restrictions are unconstitutional. It is to say that courts must subject them to the most rigid scrutiny. Pressing public necessity may sometimes justify the existence of such restrictions; racial antagonism never can. . . .

Exclusion of those of Japanese origin was deemed necessary because of the presence of an unascertained number of disloyal members of the group, most of whom we have no doubt were loyal to this country. It was because we could not reject the finding of the military authorities that it was impossible to bring about an immediate segregation of the disloyal from the loyal that we sustained the validity of the curfew order as applying to the whole group. In the instant case, temporary exclusion of the entire group was rested by the military on the same ground. The judgement that exclusion of the whole group was for the same reason a military imperative answers the contention that the exclusion was in the nature of group punishment based on antagonism to those of Japanese origin. That there were members of the group who retained loyalties in Japan has been confirmed by investigations made subsequent to the exclusion. Approximately five thousand American citizens of Japanese ancestry refused to swear unqualified allegiance to the United States and to renounce allegiance to the Japanese Emperor, and several thousand evacuees requested repatriation to Japan.

We uphold the exclusion order as of the time it was made and when the petitioner violated it. . . . In doing so, we are not unmindful of the hardships imposed by it upon a large group of American citizens. . . . But hardships are part of war, and war is an aggregation of hardships. All citizens alike, both in and out of uniform, feel the impact of war in greater or lesser measure. Citizenship has its responsibilities as well as its privileges, and in time of war the burden is always heavier. Compulsory exclusion of large groups of citizens from their homes, except under circumstances of direct emergency and peril, is inconsistent with our basic governmental institutions. But when under conditions of modern warfare our shores are threatened by hostile forces, the power to protect must be commensurate with the threatened danger. . . .

It is said that we are dealing here with the case of imprisonment of a citizen in a concentration camp solely because his ancestry, without evidence or inquiry concerning his loyalty and good disposition towards the United States. Our task would be simple, our duty clear, were this a case involving the imprisonment of a loyal citizen in a concentration camp because of racial prejudice. Regardless of the true nature of the assembly and relocation centers—and we deem it unjustifiable to call them concentration camps with all the ugly connotations that term implies—we are dealing specifically with nothing but an exclusion order. To cast this case into outlines of racial prejudice, without reference to the real military dangers which were presented, merely confuses the issue. Korematsu was not excluded from the Military Area because of hostility to him or his race. He was excluded because we are at war with the Japanese Empire, because the properly constituted military authorities feared an invasion of our West Coast and felt constrained to take proper security measures, because they decided that the military urgency of the situation demanded that all citizens of Japanese ancestry be segregated from the West Coast temporarily, and finally, because Congress, reposing its confidence in this time of war in our military leaders—as inevitably it must—

determined that they should have the power to do just this. There was evidence of disloyalty on the part of some, the military authorities considered that the need for action was great, and time was short. We cannot—by availing ourselves of the calm perspective of hindsight—now say that at that time these actions were unjustified.

Justice Murphy, dissenting.

This exclusion of "all persons of Japanese ancestry, both alien and non-alien," from the Pacific Coast area on a plea of military necessity in the absence of martial law ought not to be approved. Such exclusion goes over "the very brink of constitutional power" and falls into the ugly abyss of racism.

In dealing with matters relating to the prosecution and progress of a war, we must accord great respect and consideration to the judgments of the military authorities who are on the scene and who have full knowledge of the military facts. The scope of their discretion must, as a matter of necessity and common sense, be wide. And their judgments ought not to be overruled lightly by those whose training and duties ill-equip them to deal intelligently with matters so vital to the physical security of the nation.

At the same time, however, it is essential that there be definite limits to military discretion, especially where marital law has not been declared. Individuals must not be left impoverished of their constitutional rights on plea of military necessity that has neither substance nor support. . . .

That this forced exclusion was the result in good measure of this erroneous assumption of racial guilt rather than bona fide military necessity is evidenced by the Commanding General's Final Report on the evacuation from the Pacific Coast area. In it he refers to all individuals of Japanese descents as "subversive," as belonging to "an enemy race" whose "racial strains are undiluted," and as constituting "over 112,000 potential enemies . . . at large today" along the Pacific Coast. In support of this blanket condemnation of all persons of Japanese descent, however, no reliable evidence is cited to show that such individuals were generally disloyal, or had generally so conducted themselves in this area as to constitute a special menace to defense installations or war industries, or had otherwise by their behavior furnished reasonable ground for their exclusion as a group.

Justification for the exclusion is sought, instead, mainly upon questionable racial and sociological grounds not ordinarily within the realm of expert military judgment, supplemented by certain semi-military conclusions drawn from an unwarranted use of circumstantial evidence. . . .

No one denies, of course, that there were some disloyal persons of Japanese descent on the Pacific Coast who did all in their power to aid their ancestral land. Similar disloyal activities have been engaged in by many persons of German, Italian and even more pioneer stock in our country. But to infer that examples of individual disloyalty prove group disloyalty and justify discriminatory action against the entire group is to deny that under our system of law individual guilt is the sole basis for deprivation of rights. . . . To give constitutional sanction to that inference in this case, however well-intentioned may have been the military command on the Pacific Coast, is to adopt one of the cruelest of the rationales used by our enemies to destroy the dignity of the individual and to encourage and open the door to discriminatory actions against other minority groups in the passions of tomorrow. . . .

I dissent, therefore, from this legalization of racism. Racial discrimination in any form and in any degree has no justifiable part whatever in our democratic way of life. It is unattractive in any setting but it is utterly revolting among a free people who have embraced the principles set forth in the Constitution of the United States. All residents of this nation are kin in some way by blood or culture to a foreign land. Yet they are primarily and necessarily a part of the new and distinct civilization of the United States. They must accordingly be treated at all times as the heirs of the American experiment and as entitled to all the rights and freedoms guaranteed by the Constitution.

1. According to Judge Black, the racial prejudice suggested in the relocation was secondary to

    A. its military importance.
    B. its overall impracticality.
    C. the cooperation of the citizens.
    D. the enthusiasm of America.

2. The Commanding General's Final Report refers to Japanese Americans as

    A. "loyal American citizens."
    B. "over 112,000 regular citizens."
    C. "refugees in need of homes."
    D. "over 112,000 potential enemies."

3. About how many Japanese Americans refused to renounce their allegiance to the Japanese emperor?

    A. 1,000
    B. 5,000
    C. 10,000
    D. 50,000

4. According to Judge Black, Korematsu was excluded from the military area solely because of

    A. personal hostilities against Korematsu.
    B. prejudice against Japanese Americans.
    C. Korematsu's reputation as a criminal.
    D. the threat of invasion by Japan.

5. Justice Murphy believes that the authority of military authorities in wartime should be

    A. nonexistent.
    B. slight.
    C. wide.
    D. complete.

6. In Judge Black's statement, the curfew order was deemed valid because of the difficulty in

    A. making peace with Japan.
    B. translating peace treaties.
    C. assigning military areas.
    D. finding disloyal citizens.

7. Justice Murphy believes that Japanese Americans should not be specifically targeted because

    A. some German and Italian immigrants are also disloyal.
    B. America and Japan have had many years of cooperation.
    C. Japanese immigrants all swore allegiance to America.
    D. the curfew of Japanese communities reduced their threat.

8. What point was Justice Murphy making when he discussed the Commanding General's Final Report? Does he make a compelling argument? Use evidence from the document above to support your conclusion.

_____

_____

_____

_____

_____

_____

_____

_____

_____

_____

_____

_____

_____

_____

_____

_____

_____

_____

_____

_____

_____

_____

_____

_____

_____

GENERAL DWIGHT D. EISENHOWER'S ORDER OF THE DAY (1944)

Almost immediately after France fell to the Nazis in 1940, the Allies planned a cross-Channel assault on the German occupying forces. At the Quebec Conference in August 1943, Winston Churchill and Franklin Roosevelt reaffirmed the plan, which was code-named Overlord. Although Churchill acceded begrudgingly to the operation, historians note that the British still harbored persistent doubts about whether Overlord would succeed.

The decision to mount the invasion was cemented at the Teheran Conference held in November and December 1943. Joseph Stalin, on his first trip outside the Soviet Union since 1912, pressed Roosevelt and Churchill for details about the plan, particularly the identity of the supreme commander of Overlord. Churchill and Roosevelt told Stalin that the invasion "would be possible" by August 1, 1944, but that no decision had yet been made to name a supreme commander. To this latter point, Stalin pointedly rejoined, "Then nothing will come of these operations. Who carries the moral and technical responsibility for this operation?" Churchill and Roosevelt acknowledged the need to name the commander without further delay. Shortly after the conference ended, Roosevelt appointed General Dwight David Eisenhower to that position.

By May 1944, 2.876 million Allied troops were amassed in southern England. While awaiting deployment orders, they prepared for the assault by practicing with live ammunition. The largest armada in history, made up of more than 4,000 American, British, and Canadian ships, lay in wait. More that 1,200 planes stood ready to deliver seasoned airborne troops behind enemy lines, to silence German ground resistance as best they could, and to dominate the skies of the impending battle theater. Against a tense backdrop of uncertain weather forecasts, disagreements in strategy, and related timing dilemmas predicated on the need for optimal tidal conditions, Eisenhower decide before dawn on June 5th to proceed with Overlord. Later that same afternoon, he scribbled a note intended for release, accepting responsibility for the decision to launch the invasion and full blame should the effort to create a beachhead on the Normandy coast fail. Much more polished is his printed Order of the Day for June 6, 1944, which Eisenhower began drafting in February. The order was distributed to the 175,000-member expeditionary force on the eve of the invasion.

SUPREME HEADQUARTERS

ALLIED EXPEDITIONARY FORCE

Soldiers, Sailors, and Airmen of the Allied Expeditionary Force!

You are about to embark upon the Great Crusade, toward which we have striven these many months. The eyes of the world are upon you. The hope and prayers of liberty-loving people everywhere march with you. In company with our brave Allies and brothers-in-arms on other Fronts, you will bring about the destruction of the German war machine, the elimination of Nazi tyranny over the oppressed peoples of Europe, and security for ourselves in a free world.

Your task will not be an easy one. Your enemy is will trained, well equipped and battle-hardened. He will fight savagely.

But this is the year 1944! Much has happened since the Nazi triumphs of 1940–41. The United Nations have inflicted upon the Germans great defeats, in open battle, man-to-man. Our air offensive has seriously reduced their strength in the air and their capacity to wage war on the ground. Our Home Fronts have given us an overwhelming superiority in weapons and munitions of war, and placed at our disposal great reserves of trained fighting men. The tide has turned! The free men of the world are marching together to Victory!

I have full confidence in your courage, devotion to duty and skill in battle. We will accept nothing less than full Victory!

Good luck! And let us beseech the blessing of Almighty God upon this great and noble undertaking.

1. Which of the following **best** describes the enemy Eisenhower discusses in the document?

    A. confused and ill-equipped
    B. skilled and fierce
    C. cunning and deceitful
    D. strong and impulsive

2. Which of the following was **not** a goal of the Great Crusade?

    A. the occupation of France by American troops
    B. the destruction of the German war machine
    C. the elimination of Nazi tyranny in Europe
    D. the security for ourselves in a free world

3. According to Eisenhower, the United States reduced the enemy's strength in the air and on land with

    A. intelligence.
    B. sneak attacks.
    C. air offensive.
    D. ground offensive.

4. How does Eisenhower motivate his listeners into going to war? Support your answer with details and information from the document.

_____

_____

_____

_____

_____

_____

_____

SERVICEMEN'S READJUSTMENT ACT (1944)

While World War II was still being fought, the Department of Labor estimated that, after the war, 15 million men and women who had been serving in the armed services would be unemployed. To reduce the possibility of postwar depression brought on by widespread unemployment, the National Resources Planning Board, a White House agency, studied postwar manpower needs as early as 1942 and in June 1943 recommended a series of programs for education and training. The American Legion designed the main features of what became the Serviceman's Readjustment Act and pushed it through Congress. The bill unanimously passed both chambers of Congress in the spring of 1944. President Franklin D. Roosevelt signed it into law on June 22, 1944, just days after the D-day invasion of Normandy.

American Legion publicist Jack Cejnar called it "the GI Bill of Rights," as it offered federal aid to help veterans adjust to civilian life in the areas of hospitalization, purchase of homes and businesses, and especially, education. This act provided tuition, subsistence, books and supplies, equipment, and counseling services for veterans to continue their education in school or college. Within the following seven years, approximately 8 million veterans received educational benefits. Under the act, approximately 2.3 million attended colleges and universities, 3.5 million received school training, and 3.4 million received on-the-job training. The number of degrees awarded by U.S. colleges and universities more than doubled between 1940 and 1950, and the percentage of Americans with bachelor degrees, or advanced degrees, rose from 4.6 percent in 1945 to 25 percent a half-century later.

By 1956, when it expired, the education-and-training portion of the GI Bill had disbursed $14.5 billion to veterans—but the Veterans Administration estimated the increase in federal income taxes alone would pay for the cost of the bill several times over. By 1955, 4.3 million home loans had been granted, with a total face value of $33 billion.

In addition, veterans were responsible for buying 20 percent of all new homes built after the war. The results rippled through the rest of the economy; there would be no new depression—just unparalleled prosperity for a generation. The GI Bill has been extended several times. Nearly 2.3 million veterans participated in the program during the Korean War era and more than 8 million during the Vietnam era.

AN ACT

To provide Federal Government aid for the readjustment in civilian life of returning World War II veterans.

Be it enacted by the Senate and House of Representatives of the United States of America in Congress assembled, That this Act may be cited as the "Servicemen's Readjustment Act of 1944."

TITLE I

CHAPTER I—HOSPITALIZATION, CLAIMS, AND PROCEDURES

SEC. 100. The Veterans' Administration is hereby declared to be an essential war agency and entitled, second only to the War and Navy Departments, to priorities in personnel, equipment, supplies, and material under any laws, Executive orders, and regulations pertaining to priorities, and in appointments of personnel from civil-service registers the Administrator of Veterans' Affairs is hereby granted the same authority and discretion as the War and Navy Departments and the United States Public Health Service: Provided, That the provisions of this section as to priorities for materials shall apply to any State institution to be built for the care or hospitalization of veterans.

SEC. 101. The Administrator of Veterans' Affairs and the Federal Board of Hospitalization are hereby authorized and directed to expedite and complete the construction of additional hospital facilities for war veterans, and to enter into agreements and contracts for the use by or transfer to the Veterans' Administration of suitable Army and Navy hospitals after termination of hostilities in the present war or after such institutions are no longer needed by the armed services; and the Administrator of Veterans Affairs is hereby authorized and directed to establish necessary regional offices, sub-offices, branch offices, contact units, or other subordinate offices in centers of population where there is no Veterans' Administration facility, or where such a facility is not readily available or accessible : Provided, That there is hereby authorized to be appropriated the sum of $500,000,000 for the construction of additional hospital facilities.

SEC. 102. The Administrator of Veterans' Affairs and the Secretary of War and Secretary of the Navy are hereby granted authority to enter into agreements and contracts for the mutual use or exchange of use of hospital and domiciliary facilities, and such supplies, equipment, and material as may be needed to operate properly such facilities, or for the transfer, without reimbursement of appropriations, of facilities, supplies, equipment, or material necessary and proper for authorized care for veterans, except that at no time shall the Administrator of Veterans' Affairs enter into any agreement which will result in a permanent reduction of Veterans' Administration hospital and domiciliary beds below the number now established or approved, plus the estimated number required to meet the load of eligibles under laws administered by the Veterans' Administration, or in any way subordinate or transfer the operation of the Veterans' Administration to any other agency of the Government.

Nothing in the Selective Training and Service Act of 1940, as amended, or any other Act, shall be construed to prevent the transfer or detail of any commissioned, appointed or enlisted personnel from the armed forces to the Veterans Administration subject to agreements between the Secretary of War or the Secretary of the Navy and the Administrator of Veterans' Affairs: Provided, That no such detail shall be made or extend beyond six months after the termination of the war.

SEC. 103. The Administrator of Veterans' Affairs shall have authority to place officials and employees designated by him in such Army and Navy installations as may be deemed advisable for the purpose of adjudicating disability claims of, and giving aid and advice to, members of the Army and Navy who are about to be discharged or released from active service.

SEC. 104. No person shall be discharged or released from active duty in the armed forces until his certificate of discharge or release from active duty and final pay, or a substantial portion thereof, are ready for delivery to him or to his next of kin or legal representative; and no person shall be discharged or released from active service on account of disability until and unless he has executed a claim for compensation, pension, or hospitalization, to be filed with the Veterans' Administration or has signed a statement that he has had explained to him the right to file such claim: Provided, That this section shall not preclude immediate transfer to a veterans' facility for necessary hospital care, nor preclude the discharge of any person who refuses to sign such claim or statement: And provided further, That refusal or failure to file a claim shall be without prejudice to any right the veteran may subsequently assert.

Any person entitled to a prosthetic appliance shall be entitled, in addition, to necessary fitting and training, including institutional training, in the use of such appliance, whether in a Service or a Veterans' Administration hospital, or by out-patient treatment, including such service under contract.

SEC. 105. No person in the armed forces shall be required to sign a statement of any nature relating to the origin, incurrence, or aggravation of any disease or injury he may have, and any such statement against his own interest signed at any time, shall be null and void and of no force and effect.

1. According to the document, the Veteran's Administration may open offices

    A. in heavily populated areas.
    B. inside of Navy hospitals.
    C. in places with many veterans.
    D. in areas where there aren't any.

2. The Veteran's Administration is second only to the

    A. Federal Board of Hospitalization.
    B. War and Navy Department.
    C. Selective Training and Service Department.
    D. Senate and House of Representatives.

3. All of the following may enter into contracts to use or exchange hospital facilities and supplies **except**

    A. Secretary of War.
    B. Secretary of the Navy.
    C. Administrator of Veterans' Affairs.
    D. Speaker of the House.

4. What is the primary purpose of the Servicemen's Readjustment Act? Do you think this act served its purpose? Use information from the document to support your answer.

_____

_____

_____

_____

_____

_____

_____

_____

5. Choose one section of the act and describe its purpose.

SURRENDER OF GERMANY (1945)

The unconditional surrender of the German Third Reich was signed in the early morning hours of Monday, May 7, 1945, at Supreme Headquarters, Allied Expeditionary Force (SHAEF) at Reims in northeastern France. Present were representatives of the four Allied Powers—France, Great Britain, the Soviet Union, and the United States—and the three Germany officers delegated by German President Karl Doenitz—General Alfred Jodl, who had alone been authorized to sign the surrender document; Major Wilhelm Oxenius, an aide to Jodl; and Admiral Hans-Georg von Friedeburg, one of the German chief negotiators. Lieutenant General Walter Bedell Smith, SHAEF chief of staff, led the Allied delegation as the representative of General Eisenhower, who had refused to meet with the Germans until the surrender had been accomplished. Other American officers present were Major General Harold R. Bull and General Carl Spaatz.

After the signing of the Reims accord, Soviet chief of staff Gen. Alexei Antonov expressed concern to SHAEF that the continued fighting in the east between Germany and the Soviet Union made the Reims surrender look like a separate peace. The Soviet command wanted the Act of Military Surrender, with certain additions and alternations, to be signed at Berlin. To the Soviets, the documents signed at Berlin on May 8, 1945, represented the official, legal surrender of the Third Reich. The Berlin document had few significant changes from the one signed a day earlier at Reims.

Only this text in English is authoritative.

ACT OF MILITARY SURRENDER

We the undersigned, acting by authority of the German High Command, hereby surrender unconditionally to the Supreme Commander, Allied Expeditionary Forces and simultaneously to the Soviet High Command all forces on land, sea and in the air who are at this date under German control.

The German High Command will at once issue orders to all German military, naval and air authorties and to all forces under German control to cease active operations at 2301 hours Central European time on 8 May and to remain in the positions occupied at that time. No ship, vessel, or aircraft is to be scuttled, or any damage done to their hull, machinery or equipment.

The German High Command will at once issue to the appropriate commander, and ensure the carrying out of any further orders issued by the Supreme Commander, Allied Expeditionary Force and by the Soviet High Command.

This act of military surrender is without prejudice to, and will be superseded by any general instrument of surrender imposed by, or on behalf of the United Nations and applicable to GERMANY and the German armed forces as a whole.

In the event of the German High Command or any of the forces under their control failing to act in accordance with this Act of Surrender, the Supreme Commander, Allied Expeditionary Force and the Soviet High Command will take such punitive or other action as they deem appropriate.

Signed at RHEIMS at 0241 on the 7th day of May, 1945. France

On behalf of the German High Command,

JODL

IN THE PRESENCE OF

On behalf of the Supreme Commander,
Allied Expeditionary Force.

W.B. SMITH

On behalf of the Soviet High Command,

SOUSLOPAROV
F SEVEZ

Major General, French Army
(Witness)

1. Punitive actions may be taken against German forces that

    A. refuse to surrender.
    B. have already surrendered.
    C. defect to the Soviets.
    D. sign the Act of Surrender.

2. When German forces cease operations on May 8th, they are ordered to

    A. contact the German High Command.
    B. destroy their weaponry.
    C. report to the nearest Allied headquarters.
    D. remain in their current positions.

3. The Act of Surrender specifically warns German forces against

    A. speaking English or Russian.
    B. fraternizing with Allied soldiers.
    C. damaging their vehicles or equipment.
    D. listening to any more German orders.

4. All of the following German forces are ordered to surrender **except** _____ forces.

    A. air
    B. political
    C. ground
    D. naval

4. What will happen to Germans who refuse to surrender? Use details and information from the document to support your answer.

_____

_____

_____

_____

_____

_____

_____

_____

_____

_____

_____

_____

_____

_____

_____

_____

_____

_____

_____

_____

_____

_____

_____

_____

_____

_____

On September 2, 1945, Japanese representatives signed the official Instrument of Surrender, prepared by the War Department and approved by President Harry S Truman. It set out in eight short paragraphs the complete capitulation of Japan. The opening words, "We, acting by command of and in behalf of the Emperor of Japan," signified the importance attached to the Emperor's role by the Americans who drafted the document. The short second paragraph went straight to the heart of the matter: "We hereby proclaim the unconditional surrender to the Allied Powers of the Japanese Imperial General Headquarters and of all Japanese armed forces and all armed forces under Japanese control wherever situated."

That morning, on the deck of the USS Missouri in Tokyo Bay, the Japanese envoys Foreign Minister Mamoru Shigemitsu and General Yoshijiro Umezu signed their names on the Instrument of Surrender. The time was recorded as four minutes past 9 o'clock. Afterward, General Douglas MacArthur, Commander in the Southwest Pacific and Supreme Commander for the Allied Powers, also signed. He accepted the Japanese surrender "for the United States, Republic of China, United Kingdom, and the Union of Soviet Socialist Republics, and in the interests of the other United Nations at war with Japan."

INSTRUMENT OF SURRENDER

We, acting by command of and in behalf of the Emperor of Japan, the Japanese Government and the Japanese Imperial General Headquarters, hereby accept the provisions set forth in the declaration issued by the heads of the Governments of the United States, China, and Great Britain on 26 July 1945 at Potsdam, and subsequently adhered to by the Union of Soviet Socialist Republics, which four powers are hereafter referred to as the Allied Powers.

We hereby proclaim the unconditional surrender to the Allied Powers of the Japanese Imperial General Headquarters and of all Japanese armed forces and all armed forces under the Japanese control wherever situated.

We hereby command all Japanese forces wherever situated and the Japanese people to cease hostilites forthwith, to preserve and save from damage all ships, aircraft, and military and civil property and to comply with all requirements which may be imposed by the Supreme Commander for the Allied Powers or by agencies of the Japanese Government at his direction.

We hereby command the Japanese Imperial Headquarters to issue at once orders to the Commanders of all Japanese forces and all forces under Japanese control wherever situated to surrender unconditionally themselves and all forces under their control.

We hereby command all civil, military and naval officials to obey and enforce all proclamations, and orders and directives deemed by the Supreme Commander for the Allied Powers to be proper to effectuate this surrender and issued by him or under his authority and we direct all such officials to remain at their posts and to continue to perform their non-combatant duties unless specifically relieved by him or under his authority.

We hereby undertake for the Emperor, the Japanese Government and their successors to carry out the provisions of the Potsdam Declaration in good faith, and to issue whatever orders and take whatever actions may be required by the Supreme Commander for the Allied Poers or by any other designated representative of the Allied Powers for the purpose of giving effect to that Declaration.

We hereby command the Japanese Imperial Government and the Japanese Imperial General Headquarters at once to liberate all allied prisoners of war and civilian internees now under Japanese control and to provide for their protection, care, maintenance and immediate transportation to places as directed.

The authority of the Emperor and the Japanese Government to rule the state shall be subject to the Supreme Commander for the Allied Powers who will take such steps as he deems proper to effectuate these terms of surrender.

Signed at TOKYO BAY, JAPAN at 0904 I on the SECOND day of SEPTEMBER, 1945

MAMORU SHIGMITSU

By Command and in behalf of the Emperor
of Japan and the Japanese Government
YOSHIJIRO UMEZU

By Command and in behalf of the Japanese
Imperial General Headquarters

Accepted at TOKYO BAY, JAPAN at 0903 I on the SECOND day of SEPTEMBER, 1945, for the United States, Republic of China, United Kingdom and the Union of Soviet Socialist Republics, and in the interests of the other United Nations at war with Japan.

DOUGLAS MAC ARTHUR
Supreme Commander for the Allied Powers

C.W. NIMITZ
United States Representative

HSU YUNG-CH'ANG
Republic of China Representative

BRUCE FRASER
United Kingdom Representative

KUZMA DEREVYANKO
Union of Soviet Socialist
Republics Representative

THOMAS BLAMEY
Commonwealth of Australia
Representative

L. MOORE COSGRAVE
Dominion of Canada Representative

JACQUES LE CLERC
Provisional Government of the French
Republic Representative

C.E.L. HELFRICH
Kingdom of the Netherlands
Representative

LEONARD M. ISITT
Dominion of New Zealand Representative

1. Which of the following is **not** one of the Allied Powers?

   A. Great Britain.
   B. France.
   C. America.
   D. China.

2. Japanese officials are ordered to

   A. remain at their posts.
   B. report to Allied headquarters.
   C. retreat to Japan.
   D. meet at Potsdam.

3. This conditions of surrender were determined by

   A. General MacArthur.
   B. the emperor of Japan.
   C. the Potsdam Declaration.
   D. the Allied Powers Treaty.

4. This document orders that all Allied prisoners of war are to be

   A. liberated.
   B. identified.
   C. traded.
   D. notified.

4. According to the document, what were Japanese forces ordered to do, and what will happen to Allied prisoners of war? Use details and information from the document to support your answer.

_____

_____

_____

_____

_____

5. Why was China such an important part of the Japanese surrender process?

104

TRUMAN DOCTRINE (1947)

On Friday, February 21, 1947, the British Embassy informed the U.S. State Department officials that Great Britain could no longer provide financial aid to the governments of Greece and Turkey. American policymakers had been monitoring Greece's crumbling economic and political conditions, especially the rise of the Communist-led insurgency known as the National Liberation Front, or the EAM / ELAS. The United States had also been following events in Turkey, where a weak government faced Soviet pressure to share control of the strategic Dardanelles Strait. When Britain announced that it would withdraw aid to Greece and Turkey, the responsibility was passed on to the United States.

In a meeting between Congressmen and State Department officials, Undersecretary of State Dean Acheson articulated what would later become known as the domino theory. He stated that more was at stake than Greece and Turkey, for if those two key states should fall, communism would likely spread south to Iran and as far east as India. Acheson concluded that not since the days of Rome and Carthage had such a polarization of power existed. The stunned legislators agreed to endorse the program on the condition that President Truman stress the severity of the crisis in an address to Congress and in a radio broadcast to the American people.

Addressing a joint session of Congress on March 12, 1947, President Harry S Truman asked for $400 million in military and economic assistance for Greece and Turkey and established a doctrine, aptly characterized as the Truman Doctrine, that would guide U.S. diplomacy for the next 40 years. President Truman declared, "It must be the policy of the United States to support free peoples who are resisting attempted subjugation by armed minorities or by outside pressures." The sanction of aid to Greece and Turkey by a Republican Congress indicated the beginning of a long and enduring bipartisan cold-war foreign policy.

Mr. President, Mr. Speaker, Members of the Congress of the United States:

The gravity of the situation which confronts the world today necessitates my appearance before a joint session of the Congress. The foreign policy and the national security of this country are involved.

One aspect of the present situation, which I wish to present to you at this time for your consideration and decision, concerns Greece and Turkey.

The United States has received from the Greek Government an urgent appeal for financial and economic assistance. Preliminary reports from the American Economic Mission now in Greece and reports from the American Ambassador in Greece corroborate the statement of the Greek Government that assistance is imperative if Greece is to survive as a free nation.

I do not believe that the American people and the Congress wish to turn a deaf ear to the appeal of the Greek Government.

Greece is not a rich country. Lack of sufficient natural resources has always forced the Greek people to work hard to make both ends meet. Since 1940, this industrious and peace loving country has suffered invasion, four years of cruel enemy occupation, and bitter internal strife.

When forces of liberation entered Greece they found that the retreating Germans had destroyed virtually all the railways, roads, port facilities, communications, and merchant marine. More than a thousand villages had been burned. Eighty-five per cent of the children were tubercular. Livestock, poultry, and draft animals had almost disappeared. Inflation had wiped out practically all savings.

As a result of these tragic conditions, a militant minority, exploiting human want and misery, was able to create political chaos which, until now, has made economic recovery impossible.

Greece is today without funds to finance the importation of those goods which are essential to bare subsistence. Under these circumstances the people of Greece cannot make progress in solving their problems of reconstruction. Greece is in desperate need of financial and economic assistance to enable it to resume purchases of food, clothing, fuel and seeds. These are indispensable for the subsistence of its people and are obtainable only from abroad. Greece must have help to import the goods necessary to restore internal order and security, so essential for economic and political recovery.

The Greek Government has also asked for the assistance of experienced American administrators, economists and technicians to insure that the financial and other aid given to Greece shall be used effectively in creating a stable and self-sustaining economy and in improving its public administration.

The very existence of the Greek state is today threatened by the terrorist activities of several thousand armed men, led by Communists, who defy the government's authority at a number of points, particularly along the northern boundaries. A Commission appointed by the United Nations security Council is at present investigating disturbed conditions in northern Greece and alleged border violations along the frontier between Greece on the one hand and Albania, Bulgaria, and Yugoslavia on the other.

Meanwhile, the Greek Government is unable to cope with the situation. The Greek army is small and poorly equipped. It needs supplies and equipment if it is to restore the authority of the government throughout Greek territory. Greece must have assistance if it is to become a self-supporting and self-respecting democracy.

The United States must supply that assistance. We have already extended to Greece certain types of relief and economic aid but these are inadequate.

There is no other country to which democratic Greece can turn.

No other nation is willing and able to provide the necessary support for a democratic Greek government.

The British Government, which has been helping Greece, can give no further financial or economic aid after March 31. Great Britain finds itself under the necessity of reducing or liquidating its commitments in several parts of the world, including Greece.

We have considered how the United Nations might assist in this crisis. But the situation is an urgent one requiring immediate action and the United Nations and its related organizations are not in a position to extend help of the kind that is required.

It is important to note that the Greek Government has asked for our aid in utilizing effectively the financial and other assistance we may give to Greece, and in improving its public administration. It is of the utmost importance that we supervise the use of any funds made available to Greece; in such a manner that each dollar spent will count toward making Greece self-supporting, and will help to build an economy in which a healthy democracy can flourish.

No government is perfect. One of the chief virtues of a democracy, however, is that its defects are always visible and under democratic processes can be pointed out and corrected. The Government of Greece is not perfect. Nevertheless it represents eighty-five per cent of the members of the Greek Parliament who were chosen in an election last year. Foreign observers, including 692 Americans, considered this election to be a fair expression of the views of the Greek people.

The Greek Government has been operating in an atmosphere of chaos and extremism. It has made mistakes. The extension of aid by this country does not mean that the United States condones everything that the Greek Government has done or will do. We have condemned in the past, and we condemn now, extremist measures of the right or the left. We have in the past advised tolerance, and we advise tolerance now.

Greece's neighbor, Turkey, also deserves our attention.

The future of Turkey as an independent and economically sound state is clearly no less important to the freedom-loving peoples of the world than the future of Greece. The circumstances in which Turkey finds itself today are considerably different from those of Greece. Turkey has been spared the disasters that have beset Greece. And during the war, the United States and Great Britain furnished Turkey with material aid.

Nevertheless, Turkey now needs our support.

Since the war Turkey has sought financial assistance from Great Britain and the United States for the purpose of effecting that modernization necessary for the maintenance of its national integrity.

That integrity is essential to the preservation of order in the Middle East.

The British government has informed us that, owing to its own difficulties can no longer extend financial or economic aid to Turkey.

As in the case of Greece, if Turkey is to have the assistance it needs, the United States must supply it. We are the only country able to provide that help.

I am fully aware of the broad implications involved if the United States extends assistance to Greece and Turkey, and I shall discuss these implications with you at this time.

One of the primary objectives of the foreign policy of the United States is the creation of conditions in which we and other nations will be able to work out a way of life free from coercion. This was a fundamental issue in the war with Germany and Japan. Our victory was won over countries which sought to impose their will, and their way of life, upon other nations.

To ensure the peaceful development of nations, free from coercion, the United States has taken a leading part in establishing the United Nations, The United Nations is designed to make possible lasting freedom and independence for all its members. We shall not realize our objectives, however, unless we are willing to help free peoples to maintain their free institutions and their national integrity against aggressive movements that seek to impose upon them totalitarian regimes. This is no more than a frank recognition that totalitarian regimes imposed on free peoples, by direct or indirect aggression, undermine the foundations of international peace and hence the security of the United States.

The peoples of a number of countries of the world have recently had totalitarian regimes forced upon them against their will. The Government of the United States has made frequent protests against coercion and intimidation, in violation of the Yalta agreement, in Poland, Rumania, and Bulgaria. I must also state that in a number of other countries there have been similar developments.

At the present moment in world history nearly every nation must choose between alternative ways of life. The choice is too often not a free one.

One way of life is based upon the will of the majority, and is distinguished by free institutions, representative government, free elections, guarantees of individual liberty, freedom of speech and religion, and freedom from political oppression.

The second way of life is based upon the will of a minority forcibly imposed upon the majority. It relies upon terror and oppression, a controlled press and radio; fixed elections, and the suppression of personal freedoms.

I believe that it must be the policy of the United States to support free peoples who are resisting attempted subjugation by armed minorities or by outside pressures.

I believe that we must assist free peoples to work out their own destinies in their own way.

I believe that our help should be primarily through economic and financial aid which is essential to economic stability and orderly political processes.

The world is not static, and the status quo is not sacred. But we cannot allow changes in the status quo in violation of the Charter of the United Nations by such methods as coercion, or by such subterfuges as political infiltration. In helping free and independent nations to maintain their freedom, the United States will be giving effect to the principles of the Charter of the United Nations.

It is necessary only to glance at a map to realize that the survival and integrity of the Greek nation are of grave importance in a much wider situation. If Greece should fall under the control of an armed minority, the effect upon its neighbor, Turkey, would be immediate and serious. Confusion and disorder might well spread throughout the entire Middle East.

Moreover, the disappearance of Greece as an independent state would have a profound effect upon those countries in Europe whose peoples are struggling against great difficulties to maintain their freedoms and their independence while they repair the damages of war.

It would be an unspeakable tragedy if these countries, which have struggled so long against overwhelming odds, should lose that victory for which they sacrificed so much. Collapse of free institutions and loss of independence would be disastrous not only for them but for the world. Discouragement and possibly failure would quickly be the lot of neighboring peoples striving to maintain their freedom and independence.

Should we fail to aid Greece and Turkey in this fateful hour, the effect will be far reaching to the West as well as to the East.

We must take immediate and resolute action.

I therefore ask the Congress to provide authority for assistance to Greece and Turkey in the amount of $400,000,000 for the period ending June 30, 1948. In requesting these funds, I have taken into consideration the maximum amount of relief assistance which would be furnished to Greece out of the $350,000,000 which I recently requested that the Congress authorize for the prevention of starvation and suffering in countries devastated by the war.

In addition to funds, I ask the Congress to authorize the detail of American civilian and military personnel to Greece and Turkey, at the request of those countries, to assist in the tasks of reconstruction, and for the purpose of supervising the use of such financial and material assistance as may be furnished. I recommend that authority also be provided for the instruction and training of selected Greek and Turkish personnel.

Finally, I ask that the Congress provide authority which will permit the speediest and most effective use, in terms of needed commodities, supplies, and equipment, of such funds as may be authorized.

If further funds, or further authority, should be needed for purposes indicated in this message, I shall not hesitate to bring the situation before the Congress. On this subject the Executive and Legislative branches of the Government must work together.

This is a serious course upon which we embark.

I would not recommend it except that the alternative is much more serious. The United States contributed $341,000,000,000 toward winning World War II. This is an investment in world freedom and world peace.

The assistance that I am recommending for Greece and Turkey amounts to little more than 1 tenth of 1 per cent of this investment. It is only common sense that we should safeguard this investment and make sure that it was not in vain.

The seeds of totalitarian regimes are nurtured by misery and want. They spread and grow in the evil soil of poverty and strife. They reach their full growth when the hope of a people for a better life has died. We must keep that hope alive.

The free peoples of the world look to us for support in maintaining their freedoms.

If we falter in our leadership, we may endanger the peace of the world—and we shall surely endanger the welfare of our own nation.

Great responsibilities have been placed upon us by the swift movement of events.

I am confident that the Congress will face these responsibilities squarely.

1. The national integrity of Turkey is essential to the

    A. continuation of financing from England.
    B. preservation of order in the Middle East.
    C. safety and security of Greece.
    D. international trade of America.

2. A primary goal of American foreign policy is to

    A. make the world more like America.
    B. build a series of alliances against fascism.
    C. spread American commerce all over the world.
    D. help other nations live free of coercion.

3. In some countries, a minority imposes its will upon the majority through

    A. debate and arguments.
    B. posters and propaganda.
    C. terror and oppression.
    D. diplomacy and compromise.

4. If Greece became a Soviet state, the struggling countries of Europe would be

    A. enraged.
    B. threatened.
    C. discouraged.
    D. destroyed.

5. Truman compares his requested funding for Greece and Turkey with the

    A. cost of feeding America's poor.
    B. lives lost by the Allies in World War II.
    C. money America spent in World War II.
    D. national income of Greece and Turkey.

6. The people of Greece have to work especially hard because they

    A. support the nations around them.
    B. are situated between many groups of people.
    C. have long been ignored by Western powers.
    D. lack sufficient natural resources.

7. In the wake of German occupation, Greece was suffering all of the following **except**

    A. the world's scorn.
    B. destroyed railways.
    C. diseased children.
    D. high inflation.

8. Greece has requested the attention of all of the following groups of Americans **except**

    A. immigrants.
    B. technicians.
    C. administrators.
    D. economists.

9. The Greek parliamentary election, observed by outsiders, was considered

    A. crooked.
    B. unhelpful.
    C. unprecedented.
    D. fair.

110

10. Which two alternative ways of life does President Truman believe nations can choose between? How does America promote the better one?

_____

_____

_____

_____

_____

_____

_____

_____

_____

_____

_____

_____

_____

_____

_____

_____

_____

_____

_____

_____

_____

_____

111

EXECUTIVE ORDER 9981:
DESEGREGATION OF THE ARMED FORCES (1948)

In 1940, the U.S. population was about 131 million, 12.6 million of whom were African American, or about 10 percent of the total population. During World War II, the army had become the nation's largest minority employer. Of the 2.5 million African-American males who registered for the draft through December 31, 1945, more than one million were inducted into the armed forces. African Americans, who constituted approximately 11 per cent of all registrants liable for service, furnished approximately this proportion of the inductees in all branches of the service except the Marine Corps. Along with thousands of black women, these inductees served in all branches of service and in all Theaters of Operations during World War II.

During World War II, President Roosevelt had responded to complaints about discrimination at home against African Americans by issuing Executive Order 8802 in June 1941, directing that blacks be accepted into job-training programs in defense plants, forbidding discrimination by defense contractors, and establishing a Fair Employment Practices Commission (FEPC).

After the war, President Harry Truman, Roosevelt's successor, faced a multitude of problems and allowed Congress to terminate the FEPC. However, in December 1946, Truman appointed a distinguished panel to serve as the President's Commission on Civil Rights, which recommended "more adequate means and procedures for the protection of the civil rights of the people of the United States." When the commission issued its report, "To Secure These Rights," in October 1947, among its proposals were anti-lynching and anti-poll tax laws, a permanent FEPC, and strengthening the civil rights division of the Department of Justice.

In February 1948, President Truman called on Congress to enact all of these recommendations. When Southern Senators immediately threatened a filibuster, Truman moved ahead on civil rights by using his executive powers. Among other things, Truman bolstered the civil rights division, appointed the first African-American judge to the federal bench, named several other African Americans to high-ranking administration positions. Most importantly, on July 26, 1948, he issued an executive order abolishing segregation in the armed forces and ordering full integration of all the services. Executive Order 9981 stated that "there shall be equality of treatment and opportunity for all persons in the armed forces without regard to race, color, religion, or national origin." The order also established an advisory committee to examine the rules, practices, and procedures of the armed services and recommend ways to make desegregation a reality. There was considerable resistance to the executive order from the military, but by the end of the Korean conflict, almost all the military was integrated.

Establishing the President's Committee on Equality of Treatment and Opportunity In the Armed Forces.

WHEREAS it is essential that there be maintained in the armed services of the United States the highest standards of democracy, with equality of treatment and opportunity for all those who serve in our country's defense:

NOW THEREFORE, by virtue of the authority vested in me as President of the United States, by the Constitution and the statutes of the United States, and as Commander in Chief of the armed services, it is hereby ordered as follows:

1. It is hereby declared to be the policy of the President that there shall be equality of treatment and opportunity for all persons in the armed services without regard to race, color, religion or national origin. This policy shall be put into effect as rapidly as possible, having due regard to the time required to effectuate any necessary changes without impairing efficiency or morale.

2. There shall be created in the National Military Establishment an advisory committee to be known as the President's Committee on Equality of Treatment and Opportunity in the Armed Services, which shall be composed of seven members to be designated by the President.

3. The Committee is authorized on behalf of the President to examine into the rules, procedures and practices of the Armed Services in order to determine in what respect such rules, procedures and practices may be altered or improved with a view to carrying out the policy of this order. The Committee shall confer and advise the Secretary of Defense, the Secretary of the Army, the Secretary of the Navy, and the Secretary of the Air Force, and shall make such recommendations to the President and to said Secretaries as in the judgment of the Committee will effectuate the policy hereof.

4. All executive departments and agencies of the Federal Government are authorized and directed to cooperate with the Committee in its work, and to furnish the Committee such information or the services of such persons as the Committee may require in the performance of its duties.

5. When requested by the Committee to do so, persons in the armed services or in any of the executive departments and agencies of the Federal Governemt shall testify before the Committee and shall make available for use of the Committee such documents and other information as the Committee may require.

6. The Committee shall continue to exist until such time as the President shall terminate its existence by Executive order.

Harry Truman
The White House
July 26, 1948

1. The armed services of the United States must maintain the

   A. most efficient standards of enlistment.
   B. highest standards of democracy.
   C. toughest standards of training.
   D. most effective standards of warfare.

2. Members of the armed services are to be treated equally regardless of all of the following **except**

   A. race.
   B. color.
   C. national origin.
   D. gender.

3. The Committee on Equality of Treatment and Opportunity in the Armed Services was formed by the

    A. president.
    B. cabinet.
    C. officers of the army.
    D. Secretary of the Army.

4. The Committee's primary job is to

    A. examine military rules and procedures.
    B. enlist new recruits for the armed forces.
    C. train army officers about tactics.
    D. teach army recruiters about equality.

5. Discuss the responsibilities of the President's Committee on Equality of Treatment and Opportunity in the Armed Services. Use details and information from the document to support your answer.

Youngstown Sheet & Tube Co. v. Sawyer (1952)

If the recall of General MacArthur reaffirmed the tradition of civilian control over the military, the Steel Seizure case reminded the nation that, even in a war, the president could not act beyond the bounds of his constitutional powers.

In April 1952, President Truman ordered seizure of the nation's steel mills in order to forestall a strike which, he claimed, would have seriously harmed the nation during the Korean conflict. Although there was a law on the books, the Taft-Hartley Act, which gave the president the power to impose an eighty-day "cooling off" period when a strike was threatened, Truman refused to use that law, since he had opposed its passage in the first place. He also chose not to ask Congress for special legislation. Instead, he chose to take over control of the companies under his emergency war powers as commander-in-chief.

The steel companies did not deny that the government could take over their property in emergencies. Rather, they claimed that the wrong branch of the government had proceeded against them. In essence, they sued the president on behalf of Congress on the basis that the presidential action had violated the constitutional doctrine of separation of powers. Six members of the court agreed. Justice Hugo Black's majority opinion made a strong case for requiring the president, even in wartime, to abide by established rules.

From a constitutional standpoint, Youngstown remains one of the "great" modern cases, in that it helped to redress the balance of power among the three branches of government, a balance that had been severely distorted by the enormous growth of the executive branch and its powers first during the Great Depression, then during the war and the subsequent postwar search for global security.

Justice Black delivered the opinion of the Court.

We are asked to decide whether the President . . . was acting within his constitutional power when he issued an order directing the Secretary of Commerce to take possession of and operate most of the Nation's steel mills. The mill owners argued that the President's order amounts to lawmaking, a legislative function which the Constitution has expressly confided to the Congress and not to the President. The Government's position is that the order was made on findings of the President that his action was necessary to avert a national catastrophe which would inevitably result from a stoppage of steel production, and that in meeting this grave emergency the President was acting within the aggregate of his constitutional powers as the Nation's Chief Executive and the Commander in Chief of the Armed Forces of the United States. . . .

The President's power, if any, to issue the order must stem either from an act of Congress or from the Constitution itself. There is no statute that expressly authorizes the President to take possession of property as he did here. Nor is there any act of Congress to which our attention has been directed from which such a power can fairly be implied. There are two statutes which do authorize the President to take both personal and real property under certain conditions . . . .However, the Government admits that these conditions were not met and that the President's order was not rooted in either of the statutes. . . .

Moreover, the use of the seizures technique to solve labor disputes in order to prevent work stoppages was not only unauthorized by any congressional enactment; prior to this controversy, Congress had refused to adopt that method of settling labor disputes. When the Taft-Hartley Act was under consideration in 1947, Congress rejected an amendment which would have authorized such governmental seizures in cases of emergency. Instead, the plan sought to bring about settlements by use of the customary devices of mediation, conciliation, investigations by boards of inquiry, and public reports. In some instances temporary injunctions were authorized to provide cooling-off periods. All this failing, unions were left free to strike. . . .

It is clear that if the president had authority to issue the order he did, it must be found in some provision of the Constitution. And it is not claimed that express constitutional language grants this power to the President. The contention is that presidential power should be implied from the aggregate of his powers under the Constitution. Particular reliance is placed on provisions in Article II which say that "The executive Power shall be vested in a President"; that "he shall take Care that the Laws be faithfully executed"; and that he "shall be Commander in Chief of the Army and Navy of the United States."

The order cannot properly be sustained as an exercise of the President's military power as Commander in Chief of the Armed Forces. The Government attempts to do so by citing a number of cases upholding broad powers in military commanders engaged in day-to-day fighting in a theater of war. Such cases need not concern us here. Even though "theater of war" be an expanding concept, we cannot with faithfulness to our constitutional system hold that the Commander in Chief of the Armed Forces has the ultimate power as such to take possession of private property in order to keep labor disputes from stopping production. This is a job for the Nation's lawmakers, not for its military authorities.

Nor can the seizure order be sustained because of the several constitutional provisions that grant executive power to the President. In the framework of our Constitution, the President's power to see that the laws are faithfully executed refutes the idea that he is to be a lawmaker. The Constitution limits his functions in the law-making process to the recommending of laws he thinks wise and the vetoing of laws he thinks bad. And the Constitution is neither silent nor equivocal about who shall make laws which the President is to execute. . . .

The President's order does not direct that a congressional policy be executed in a manner prescribed by Congress—it directs that a presidential policy be executed in a manner prescribed by the President. The preamble of the order itself, like that of many statutes, sets out reasons why the President believes certain policies should be adopted, proclaims these policies as rules of conduct to be followed, and again, like a statute, authorizes a government official to promulgate additional rules and regulations consistent with the policy proclaimed and needed to carry that policy into execution. The power of Congress to adopt such public policies as those proclaimed by the order is beyond question. It can authorize the taking of private property for public use. It can make laws regulating the relationships between employers and employees, prescribing rules designed to settle labor disputes, and fixing wages and working conditions in certain fields of our economy. The Constitution does not subject this lawmaking power of Congress to presidential or military supervision or control.

It is said that other Presidents without congressional authority have taken possession of private business enterprises in order to settle labor disputes. But even if this be true, Congress has not thereby lost its exclusive constitutional authority to make laws necessary and proper to carry out the powers vested by the Constitution "in the Government of the United States, or any Department or Officer thereof."

The Founders of this Nation entrusted the lawmaking power to the Congress alone in both good and bad times. It would do no good to recall the historical events, the fears of power and the hopes for freedom that lay behind their choice. Such a review would but confirm our holding that this seizure order cannot stand.

1. *Youngstown Sheet & Tube Co.* v. *Sawyer* occurred after President Truman ordered the Secretary of Commerce to

    A. shut down steel mills.
    B. negotiate labor disputes in steel mills.
    C. raise the salary of workers in steel mills.
    D. take possession of steel mills.

2. Steel mill owners accused the president of

    A. lawmaking.
    B. corruption.
    C. monopolizing an industry.
    D. increasing competition.

3. If the president had the power to seize steel mills, that power must be outlined in

    A. appellate court rulings.
    B. the Constitution or legislation.
    C. polls of voters.
    D. an executive order.

4. Why did the president make his controversial decision?

    A. to punish industry leaders
    B. to force desegregation
    C. to avert a steel shortage
    D. to end the Korean War

5. The Taft-Hartley Act allowed for labor settlements by all of the following methods **except**

    A. conciliation.
    B. public reports.
    C. government seizure.
    D. mediation.

6. Why does the Supreme Court rule the way it does? Do you agree with its ruling?

_____

_____

_____

_____

_____

_____

_____

_____

_____

_____

_____

_____

_____

_____

_____

_____

_____

_____

_____

_____

_____

_____

_____

_____

_____

_____

ARMISTICE AGREEMENT FOR KOREA STATE (1953)

The Korean War, which began on June 25, 1950, when the North Koreans invaded South Korea, officially ended on July 27, 1953. At 10 a.m., in Panmunjom, scarcely acknowledging each other, U.S. Army Lieutenant General William K. Harrison, Jr., senior delegate, United Nations Command Delegation; North Korean General Nam Il, senior delegate, Delegation of the Korean People's Army and the Chinese People's Volunteers, signed eighteen official copies of the tri-language Korean Armistice Agreement.

It was the end of the longest negotiated armistice in history: 158 meetings spread over two years and 17 days. That evening at 10 p.m., the truce went into effect. The Korean Armistice Agreement is somewhat exceptional in that it is purely a military document—no nation is a signatory to the agreement. Specifically the Armistice Agreement:

1. *suspended open hostilities;*

2. *withdrew all military forces and equipment from a 4,000-meter-wide zone, establishing the Demilitarized Zone as a buffer between the forces;*

3. *prevented both sides from entering the air, ground, or sea areas under control of the other;*

4. *arranged release and repatriation of prisoners of war and displaced persons; and*

5. *established the Military Armistice Commission (MAC) and other agencies to discuss any violations and to ensure adherence to the truce terms.*

While it stopped hostilities, the armistice was not a permanent peace treaty between nations.

President Eisenhower, who was keenly aware of the 1.8 million American men and women who had served in Korea and the 36,576 Americans who had died there, played a key role in bringing about a cease-fire. In announcing the agreement to the American people in a television address shortly after the signing, he said, in part:

Soldiers, sailors and airmen of sixteen different countries have stood as partners beside us throughout these long and bitter months. In this struggle we have seen the United Nations meet the challenge of aggression—not with pathetic words of protest, but with deeds of decisive purpose. And so at long last the carnage of war is to cease and the negotiation of the conference table is to begin. . . . [We hope that] all nations may come to see the wisdom of composing differences in this fashion before, rather than after, there is resort to brutal and futile battle.

Now as we strive to bring about that wisdom, there is, in this moment of sober satisfaction, one thought that must discipline our emotions and steady our resolution. It is this: We have won an armistice on a single battleground—not peace in the world. We may not now relax our guard nor cease our quest.

July 27, 1953

Agreement between the Commander-in-Chief, United Nations Command, on the one hand, and the Supreme Commander of the Korean People's Army and the Commander of the Chinese People's volunteers, on the other hand, concerning a military armistice in Korea.

Preamble

The undersigned, the Commander-in-Chief, United Nations Command, on the one hand, and the Supreme Commander of the Korean People's Army and the Commander of the Chinese People's Volunteers, on the other hand, in the interest of stopping the Korean conflict, with its great toil of suffering and bloodshed on both sides, and with the objective of establishing an armistice which will insure a complete cessation of hostilities and of all acts of armed force in Korea until a final peaceful settlement is achieved, do individually, collectively, and mutually agree to accept and to be bound and governed by the conditions and terms of armistice set forth in the following articles and paragraphs, which said conditions and terms are intended to be purely military in character and to pertain solely to the belligerents in Korea:

Article I

Military Demarcation Line and Demilitarized Zone

1. A military demarcation line shall be fixed and both sides shall withdraw two (2) kilometers from this line so as to establish a demilitarized zone between the opposing forces. A demilitarized zone shall be established as a buffer zone to prevent the occurrence of incidents which might lead to a resumption of hostilities.

2. The military demarcation line is located as indicated on the attached map.

3. This demilitarized zone is defined by a northern and southern boundary as indicated on the attached map.

4. The military demarcation line shall be plainly marked as directed by the Military Armistice Commission hereinafter established. The Commanders of the opposing sides shall have suitable markers erected along the boundary between the demilitarized zone and their respective areas. The Military Armistice Commission shall supervise the erection of all markers placed along the military demarcation line and along the boundaries of the demilitarized zone.

5. The waters of the Han River Estuary shall be open to civil shipping of both sides wherever one bank is controlled by one side and the other bank is controlled by the other side. The Military Armistice Commission shall prescribe rules for the shipping in that part of the Han River Estuary indicated on the attached map. Civil shipping of each side shall have unrestricted access to the land under the military control of that side.

6. Neither side shall execute any hostile act within, from, or against the demilitarized zone.

7. No person, military or civilian, shall be permitted to cross the military demarcation line unless specifically authorized to do so by the Military Armistice Commission.

8. No, person military of civilian, in the demilitarized zone shall be permitted to enter the territory under the military control of either side unless specifically authorized to do so by the Commander into whose territory entry is sought.

9. No person, military or civilian, shall be permitted to enter the demilitarized zone except persons concerned with the conduct of civil administration and relief and persons specifically authorized to enter by the Military Armistice Commission . . .

Done at Panmunjom, Korea at 10:00 hours on the 27th day of July 1953, in English, Korean and Chinese, all texts being equally authentic.
NAM IL

_____

General, Korea People's Army
Senior Delegate,
Delegation of the Korean People's Army
and the Chinese People's Volunteers
WILLIAM K. HARRISON, JR.

_____

Lieutenant General, United States Army
Senior Delegate,
United Nations Command Delegation

1. The primary goal of the armistice agreement was to

    A. end the conflict in Korea permanently.
    B. stop hostilities until a final settlement is reached.
    C. establish the Military Armistice Commission.
    D. delineate the boundaries between opposing forces.

2. The width of the demilitarized zone is

    A. one kilometer.
    B. two kilometers.
    C. five kilometers.
    D. ten kilometers.

3. The boundaries of the demilitarized zone will be clarified using

    A. fortresses.
    B. armed guards.
    C. stone walls.
    D. markers.

4. Parts of the Han River Estuary that pass between the opponents' territories will be

    A. open to civilian shipping.
    B. closed to civilian shipping.
    C. patrolled by the United Nations.
    D. surrendered to the Chinese.

5. The armistice is described as being

    A. acknowledge only by Americans.
    B. accepted by all nations involved.
    C. purely military in character.
    D. purely civilian in character.

6. What was the purpose of the demarcation zone? Use details and information from the document to support your answer.

_____

_____

_____

_____

_____

_____

_____

_____

_____

_____

_____

_____

_____

_____

_____

_____

_____

_____

_____

_____

_____

_____

_____

SENATE RESOLUTION 301:
CENSURE OF SENATOR JOSEPH MCCARTHY (1954)

The early years of the Cold War saw the United States facing a hostile Soviet Union, the "loss" of China to communism, and war in Korea. In this politically charged atmosphere, fears of Communist influence over American institutions spread easily. On February 9, 1950, Joseph McCarthy, a Republican Senator from Wisconsin, claimed that he had a list of 205 State Department employees who were Communists. While he offered little proof, the claims gained the Senator great notoriety. In June, Senator Margaret Chase Smith of Maine and six fellow Republicans issued a "Declaration of Conscience" asserting that because of McCarthy's tactics, the Senate had been "debased to the level of a forum for hate and character assassination." However, McCarthy took advantage of the Cold War atmosphere of fear and suspicion and with strong support in the opinion polls, McCarthy's attacks and interventions in senatorial elections brought defeat to some of his party's Democratic opponents.

After Republicans took control of the White House and Congress in 1953, McCarthy was named chairman of the Committee on Government Operations and its Subcommittee on Investigations. From these posts, he continued to accuse government agencies of being "soft" on communism, but he was now attacking a Republican administration. In 1954, McCarthy's investigation of security threats in the U.S. Army was televised. McCarthy's bullying of witnesses turned public opinion against the senator. On December 2, 1954, the Senate voted to censure him, describing his behavior as "contrary to senatorial traditions."

Republican Senators Ralph Flanders of Vermont, Arthur Watkins of Utah, and Margaret Chase Smith of Maine led the efforts to discipline McCarthy. Flanders introduced two separate resolutions against McCarthy, one removing McCarthy from his chairmanships and the other calling for his censure. The censure resolution moved forward with debate beginning July 30, 1954. The full Senate took up the resolution on November 5th. This copy of the resolution catches the debate on November 9th as the Senate refined the wording of its resolution. The substance of the first count, charging McCarthy with failure to cooperate with a Senate subcommittee, remained unchanged in the final resolution. The second count was dropped for a condemnation of McCarthy's attacks on the very members of the committee that considered his censure.

Resolved, That the Senator from Wisconsin, Mr. McCarthy, failed to cooperate with the Subcommittee on Privileges and Elections of the Senate Committee on Rules and Administration in clearing up matters referred to that subcommittee which concerned his conduct as a Senator and affected the honor of the Senate and, instead, repeatedly abused the subcommittee and its members who were trying to carry out assigned duties, thereby obstructing the constitutional processes of the Senate, and that this conduct of the Senator from Wisconsin, Mr. McCarthy, is contrary to senatorial traditions and is hereby condemned.

Sec 2. The Senator from Wisconsin, Mr. McCarthy, in writing to the chairman of the Select Committee to Study Censure Charges (Mr. Watkins) after the Select Committee had issued its report and before the report was presented to the Senate charging three members of the Select Committee with "deliberate deception" and "fraud" for failure to disqualify themselves; in stating to the press on November 4, 1954, that the special Senate session that was to begin November 8, 1954, was a "lynch-party"; in repeatedly describing this special Senate session as a "lynch bee" in a nationwide television and radio show on November 7, 1954; in stating to the public press on November 13, 1954, that the chairman of the Select Committee (Mr. Watkins) was guilty of "the most unusual, most cowardly things I've ever heard of" and stating further: "I expected he would be afraid to answer the questions, but didn't think he'd be stupid enough to make a public statement"; and in characterizing the said committee as the "unwitting handmaiden," "involuntary agent" and "attorneys-in-fact" of the Communist Party and in charging that the said committee in writing its report "imitated Communist methods—that it distorted, misrepresented, and omitted in its effort to manufacture a plausible rationalization" in support of its recommendations to the Senate, which characterizations and charges were contained in a statement released to the press and inserted in the Congressional Record of November 10, 1954, acted contrary to senatorial ethics and tended to bring the Senate into dishonor and disrepute, to obstruct the constitutional processes of the Senate, and to impair its dignity; and such conduct is hereby condemned.

1. According to this document, Senator McCarthy referred to the November 8, 1954, Senate session as

   A. a "deliberate deceit."
   B. an "unethical tradition."
   C. a "distorted rationalization."
   D. a "lynch-party."

2. McCarthy became most famous for accusing government officials of being

   A. liars and cowards.
   B. robbers and hoarders.
   C. Communist sympathizers.
   D. Fascist sympathizers.

3. The Select Committee to Study Censure Charges was characterized by McCarthy as being

   A. patriotic.
   B. crooked.
   C. ethical.
   D. tyrannical.

4. The conduct of McCarthy was condemned by the Senate for all of the following reasons **except** that it

   A. brought dishonor to the Senate.
   B. obstructed constitutional processes.
   C. impaired the Senate's dignity
   D. reduced the government's power.

5. In what way did McCarthy obstruct justice? Use details and information from the document to support your answer.

_____

_____

_____

_____

_____

_____

_____

_____

_____

_____

_____

_____

_____

_____

_____

_____

_____

_____

_____

_____

_____

_____

BROWN V. BOARD OF EDUCATION (1954)

On May 17, 1954, U.S. Supreme Court Justice Earl Warren delivered the unanimous ruling in the landmark civil rights case Brown v. *Board of Education of Topeka, Kansas. State-sanctioned segregation of public schools was a violation of the 14th amendment and was therefore unconstitutional. This historic decision marked the end of the "separate but equal" precedent set by the Supreme Court nearly 60 years earlier in* Plessy v. *Ferguson and served as a catalyst for the expanding civil rights movement during the decade of the 1950s.*

Arguments were to be heard during the next term to determine just how the ruling would be imposed. Just over one year later, on May 31, 1955, Warren read the court's unanimous decision—now referred to as Brown II—*instructing the states to begin desegregation plans "with all deliberate speed."*

Despite two unanimous decisions and careful, if vague, wording, there was considerable resistance to the Supreme Court's ruling in Brown v. *Board of Education. In addition to the obvious disapproving segregationists were some constitutional scholars who felt that the decision went against legal tradition by relying heavily on data supplied by social scientists rather than precedent or established law. Supporters of judicial restraint believed the court had overstepped its constitutional powers by essentially writing new law.*

However, minority groups and members of the civil rights movement were buoyed by the Brown *decision even without specific directions for implementation. Proponents of judicial activism believed the Supreme Court had appropriately used its position to adapt the basis of the Constitution to address new problems in new times. The Warren Court stayed this course for the next 15 years, deciding cases that significantly affected not only race relations, but also the administration of criminal justice, the operation of the political process, and the separation of church and state.*

SUPREME COURT OF THE UNITED STATES

Brown v. Board of Education, 347 U.S. 483 (1954) (USSC+)
Argued December 9, 1952
Reargued December 8, 1953
Decided May 17, 1954
APPEAL FROM THE UNITED STATES DISTRICT COURT FOR THE DISTRICT OF KANSAS*

Opinion

MR. CHIEF JUSTICE WARREN delivered the opinion of the Court.

These cases come to us from the States of Kansas, South Carolina, Virginia, and Delaware. They are premised on different facts and different local conditions, but a common legal question justifies their consideration together in this consolidated opinion.

In each of the cases, minors of the Negro race, through their legal representatives, seek the aid of the courts in obtaining admission to the public schools of their community on a nonsegregated basis. In each instance, they had been denied admission to schools attended by white children under laws requiring or permitting segregation according to race. This segregation was alleged to deprive the plaintiffs of the equal protection of the laws under the Fourteenth Amendment. In each of the cases other than the Delaware case, a three-judge federal district court denied relief to the plaintiffs on the so-called "separate but equal" doctrine announced by this Court in *Plessy* v. *Ferguson*, 163 U.S. 537. Under that doctrine, equality of treatment is accorded when the races are provided substantially equal facilities, even though these facilities be separate. In the Delaware case, the Supreme Court of Delaware adhered to that doctrine, but ordered that the plaintiffs be admitted to the white schools because of their superiority to the Negro schools.

The plaintiffs contend that segregated public schools are not "equal" and cannot be made "equal," and that hence they are deprived of the equal protection of the laws. Because of the obvious importance of the question presented, the Court took jurisdiction. Argument was heard in the 1952 Term, and reargument was heard this Term on certain questions propounded by the Court.

Reargument was largely devoted to the circumstances surrounding the adoption of the Fourteenth Amendment in 1868. It covered exhaustively consideration of the Amendment in Congress, ratification by the states, then-existing practices in racial segregation, and the views of proponents and opponents of the Amendment. This discussion and our own investigation convince us that, although these sources cast some light, it is not enough to resolve the problem with which we are faced. At best, they are inconclusive. The most avid proponents of the post-War Amendments undoubtedly intended them to remove all legal distinctions among "all persons born or naturalized in the United States." Their opponents, just as certainly, were antagonistic to both the letter and the spirit of the Amendments and wished them to have the most limited effect. What others in Congress and the state legislatures had in mind cannot be determined with any degree of certainty. An additional reason for the inconclusive nature of the Amendment's history with respect to segregated schools is the status of public education at that time. In the South, the movement toward free common schools, supported by general taxation, had not yet taken hold. Education of white children was largely in the hands of private groups. Education of Negroes was almost nonexistent, and practically all of the race were illiterate. In fact, any education of Negroes was forbidden by law in some states. Today, in contrast, many Negroes have achieved outstanding success in the arts and sciences, as well as in the business and professional world. It is true that public school education at the time of the Amendment had advanced further in the North, but the effect of the Amendment on Northern States was generally ignored in the congressional debates. Even in the North, the conditions of public education did not approximate those existing today. The curriculum was usually rudimentary; ungraded schools were common in rural areas; the school term was but three months a year in many states, and compulsory school attendance was virtually unknown. As a consequence, it is not surprising that there should be so little in the history of the Fourteenth Amendment relating to its intended effect on public education.

In the first cases in this Court construing the Fourteenth Amendment, decided shortly after its adoption, the Court interpreted it as proscribing all state-imposed discriminations against the Negro race. The doctrine of "separate but equal" did not make its appearance in this Court until 1896 in the case of *Plessy* v. *Ferguson*, supra, involving not education but transportation. American courts have since labored with the doctrine for over half a century. In this Court, there have been six cases involving the "separate but equal" doctrine in the field of public education. In *Cumming* v. *County Board of Education*, 175 U.S. 528, and *Gong Lum* v. *Rice*, 275 U.S. 78, the validity of the doctrine itself was not challenged. In more recent cases, all on the graduate school level, inequality was found in that specific benefits enjoyed by white students were denied to Negro students of the same educational qualifications. *Missouri ex rel. Gaines* v. *Canada*, 305 U.S. 337; *Sipuel* v. *Oklahoma*, 332 U.S. 631; *Sweatt* v. *Painter*, 339 U.S. 629; *McLaurin* v. *Oklahoma State Regents*, 339 U.S. 637. In none of these cases was it necessary to reexamine the doctrine to grant relief to the Negro plaintiff. And in *Sweatt* v. *Painter*, supra, the Court expressly reserved decision on the question whether *Plessy* v. *Ferguson* should be held inapplicable to public education.

In the instant cases, that question is directly presented. Here, unlike Sweatt v. Painter, there are findings below that the Negro and white schools involved have been equalized, or are being equalized, with respect to buildings, curricula, qualifications and salaries of teachers, and other "tangible" factors. Our decision, therefore, cannot turn on merely a comparison of these tangible factors in the Negro and white schools involved in each of the cases. We must look instead to the effect of segregation itself on public education.

In approaching this problem, we cannot turn the clock back to 1868, when the Amendment was adopted, or even to 1896, when *Plessy* v. *Ferguson* was written. We must consider public education in the light of its full development and its present place in American life throughout the Nation. Only in this way can it be determined if segregation in public schools deprives these plaintiffs of the equal protection of the laws.

Today, education is perhaps the most important function of state and local governments. Compulsory school attendance laws and the great expenditures for education both demonstrate our recognition of the importance of education to our democratic society. It is required in the performance of our most basic public responsibilities, even service in the armed forces. It is the very foundation of good citizenship. Today it is a principal instrument in awakening the child to cultural values, in preparing him for later professional training, and in helping him to adjust normally to his environment. In these days, it is doubtful that any child may reasonably be expected to succeed in life if he is denied the opportunity of an education. Such an opportunity, where the state has undertaken to provide it, is a right which must be made available to all on equal terms.
We come then to the question presented: Does segregation of children in public schools solely on the basis of race, even though the physical facilities and other "tangible" factors may be equal, deprive the children of the minority group of equal educational opportunities? We believe that it does.

In *Sweatt* v. *Painter*, supra, in finding that a segregated law school for Negroes could not provide them equal educational opportunities, this Court relied in large part on "those qualities which are incapable of objective measurement but which make for greatness in a law school." In *McLaurin* v. *Oklahoma State Regents*, supra, the Court, in requiring that a Negro admitted to a white graduate school be treated like all other students, again resorted to intangible considerations: " . . . his ability to study, to engage in discussions and exchange views with other students, and, in general, to learn his profession." Such considerations apply with added force to children in grade and high schools. To separate them from others of similar age and qualifications solely because of their race generates a feeling of inferiority as to their status in the community that may affect their hearts and minds in a way unlikely ever to be undone. The effect of this separation on their educational opportunities was well stated by a finding in the Kansas case by a court which nevertheless felt compelled to rule against the Negro plaintiffs:

Segregation of white and colored children in public schools has a detrimental effect upon the colored children. The impact is greater when it has the sanction of the law, for the policy of separating the races is usually interpreted as denoting the inferiority of the negro group. A sense of inferiority affects the motivation of a child to learn. Segregation with the sanction of law, therefore, has a tendency to [retard] the educational and mental development of negro children and to deprive them of some of the benefits they would receive in a racial[ly] integrated school system.

Whatever may have been the extent of psychological knowledge at the time of *Plessy* v. *Ferguson*, this finding is amply supported by modern authority. Any language in *Plessy* v. *Ferguson* contrary to this finding is rejected.

We conclude that, in the field of public education, the doctrine of "separate but equal" has no place. Separate educational facilities are inherently unequal. Therefore, we hold that the plaintiffs and others similarly situated for whom the actions have been brought are, by reason of the segregation complained of, deprived of the equal protection of the laws guaranteed by the Fourteenth Amendment. This disposition makes unnecessary any discussion whether such segregation also violates the Due Process Clause of the Fourteenth Amendment.

Because these are class actions, because of the wide applicability of this decision, and because of the great variety of local conditions, the formulation of decrees in these cases presents problems of considerable complexity. On reargument, the consideration of appropriate relief was necessarily subordinated to the primary question—the constitutionality of segregation in public education. We have now announced that such segregation is a denial of the equal protection of the laws. In order that we may have the full assistance of the parties in formulating decrees, the cases will be restored to the docket, and the parties are requested to present further argument on Questions 4 and 5 previously propounded by the Court for the reargument this Term The Attorney General of the United States is again invited to participate. The Attorneys General of the states requiring or permitting segregation in public education will also be permitted to appear as amici curiae upon request to do so by September 15, 1954, and submission of briefs by October 1, 1954.

It is so ordered.

* Together with No. 2, *Briggs et al.* v. *Elliott et al.*, on appeal from the United States District Court for the Eastern District of South Carolina, argued December 9–10, 1952, reargued December 7–8, 1953; No. 4, *Davis et al.* v. *County School Board of Prince Edward County, Virginia, et al.*, on appeal from the United States District Court for the Eastern District of Virginia, argued December 10, 1952, reargued December 7–8, 1953, and No. 10, *Gebhart et al.* v. *Belton et al.*, on certiorari to the Supreme Court of Delaware, argued December 11, 1952, reargued December 9, 1953.

1. Cases relating to segregation in public schools have come to the court from all of the following states **except**

    A. Virginia.
    B. Arkansas.
    C. Kansas.
    D. South Carolina.

2. Segregation in public schools was deemed a violation of which constitutional amendment?

    A. the fourteenth amendment
    B. the fifteenth amendment
    C. the sixteenth amendment
    D. the seventeenth amendment

3. The *Plessy* v. *Ferguson* case established which of the following doctrines?

    A. "due process clause"
    B. "separation of church and state"
    C. "pursuit of happiness"
    D. "separate but equal"

4. What was a primary difference between southern public schools in 1868 and those of 1954?

    A. Southern schools were run by northern administrators in 1868.
    B. No children of any race received organized educated in 1868.
    C. Free public schools, supported by taxes, were rare in 1868.
    D. All children, regardless of color, were given free education in 1868.

5. Legal public school segregation is harmful to black children even if the physical facilities are equal because

    A. transportation to segregated schools is difficult.
    B. the laws suggest to blacks that they are inferior.
    C. teachers in blacks-only schools are less qualified.
    D. students are discouraged from learning the laws.

6. According to the document, the *Brown* case is especially complex for all of the following reasons **except**

    A. the ruling would apply to many people.
    B. the local conditions of the schools vary.
    C. most blacks did not want desegregation.
    D. many administrators will resist the ruling.

7. Each related case brought before the court was prompted by

    A. school administrators seeking to continue segregation.
    B. black youths seeking to enroll in public schools.
    C. legal analysts seeking to study race relations in the South.
    D. lawmakers hoping to update constitutional amendments.

8. In this document, the court is ruling

    A. for segregation nationwide.
    B. for segregation in the south.
    C. against segregation nationwide.
    D. against segregation in the south.

9. Why did the Fourteenth Amendment have so little to say about public education? How had that situation changed by 1954, and how is it different today?

_____

_____

_____

_____

_____

_____

_____

_____

_____

_____

_____

_____

_____

_____

_____

_____

_____

_____

_____

_____

_____

_____

_____

_____

_____

131

National Interstate and Defense Highways Act (1956)

Popularly known as the National Interstate and Defense Highways Act of 1956, the Federal-Aid Highway Act of 1956 established an interstate highway system in the United States. The movement behind the construction of a transcontinental superhighway started in the 1930s when President Franklin D. Roosevelt expressed interest in the construction of a network of toll superhighways that would provide more jobs for people in need of work during the Great Depression. The resulting legislation was the Federal-Aid Highway Act of 1938. It directed the chief of the Bureau of Public Roads (BPR) to study the feasibility of a six-route toll network. But with America on the verge of joining the war in Europe, the time for a massive highway program had not arrived. At the end of the war, the Federal-Aid Highway Act of 1944 funded highway improvements. It established major new ground by authorizing and designating, in Section 7, the construction of 40,000 miles of a "National System of Interstate Highways."

When President Dwight D. Eisenhower took office in January 1953, however, the states had only completed 6,500 miles of the system improvements. Eisenhower had first realized the value of good highways in 1919, when he participated in the U.S. Army's first transcontinental motor convoy from Washington, DC, to San Francisco. Again, during World War II, Eisenhower saw the German advantage that resulted from their autobahn highway network. He also noted the enhanced mobility of the Allies, on those same highways, when they fought their way into Germany. These experiences significantly shaped Eisenhower's views on highways and their role in national defense. During his State of the Union Address on January 7, 1954, Eisenhower made it clear that he was ready to turn his attention to the nation's highway problems. He considered it important to "protect the vital interest of every citizen in a safe and adequate highway system."

Between 1954 and 1956, there were several failed attempts to pass a national highway bill through the Congress. The main controversy over the highway construction was the apportionment of the funding between the federal government and the states. Undaunted, the president renewed his call for a "modern, interstate highway system" in his 1956 State of the Union Address. Within a few months, after considerable debate and amendment in the Congress, The Federal-Aid Highway Act of 1956 emerged from the House-Senate conference committee. In the act, the interstate system was expanded to 41,000 miles. To construct the network, $25 billion was authorized for fiscal years 1957 through 1969. During his recovery from a minor illness, Eisenhower signed the bill into law at Walter Reed Army Medical Center on the June 29th. Because of the 1956 law, and the subsequent Highway Act of 1958, the pattern of community development in America was fundamentally altered. It was based on the automobile.

AN ACT

To amend and supplement the Federal-Aid Road Act approved July 11, 1916, to authorize appropriations for continuing the construction of highways; to amend the Internal Revenue Code of 1954 to provide additional revenue from the taxes on motor fuel, tires, and trucks and buses; and for other purposes.

Be it enacted by the Senate and House of Representatives of the United States of America in Congress assembled,

TITLE I—FEDERAL-AID HIGHWAY ACT OF 1956

SEC. 101. SHORT TITLE FOR TITLE I.
This title may be cited as the "Federal-Aid Highway Act of 1956."

SEC. 102. FEDERAL-AID HIGHWAYS.

(a) (1) AUTHORIZATION OF APPROPRIATIONS.—For the purpose of carrying out the provisions of the Federal-Aid Road Act approved July 11, 1916 (39 Stat. 355), and all Acts amendatory thereof and supplementary thereto, there is hereby authorized to be appropriated for the fiscal year ending June 30, 1957, $125,000,000 in addition to any sums heretofore authorized for such fiscal year; the sum of $850,000,000 for the fiscal year ending June 30, 1958; and the sum of $875,000,000 for the fiscal year ending June 30, 1959. The sums herein authorized for each fiscal year shall be available for expenditure as follows:

(A) 45 per centum for projects on the Federal-aid primary high-way system.

(B) 30 per centum for projects on the Federal-aid secondary high-way system.

(C) 25 per centum for projects on extensions of these systems within urban areas.

(2) APPORTIONMENTS.—The sums authorized by this section shall be apportioned among the several States in the manner now provided by law and in accordance with the formulas set forth in section 4 of the Federal-Aid Highway Act of 1944; approved December 20, 1944 (58 Stat. 838) : Provided, That the additional amount herein authorized for the fiscal year ending June 30, 1957, shall be apportioned immediately upon enactment of this Act.

(b) AVAILABILITY FOR EXPENDITURE.—Any sums apportioned to any State under this section shall be available for expenditure in that State for two years after the close of the fiscal year for which such sums are authorized, and any amounts so apportioned remaining unexpended at the end of such period shall lapse: Provided, That such funds shall be deemed to have been expended if a sum equal to the total of the sums herein and heretofore apportioned to the State is covered by formal agreements with the Secretary of Commerce for construction, reconstruction, or improvement of specific projects as provided in this title and prior Acts: Provided further, That in the case of those sums heretofore, herein, or hereafter apportioned to any State for projects on the Federal-aid secondary highway system, the Secretary of Commerce may, upon the request of any State, discharge his responsibility relative to the plans, specifications, estimates, surveys, contract awards, design, inspection, and construction of such secondary road projects by his receiving and approving a certified statement by the State highway department setting forth that the plans, design, and construction for such projects are in accord with the standards and procedures of such State applicable . . .

SEC. 108. NATIONAL SYSTEM OF INTERSTATE AND DEFENSE HIGHWAYS.

(a) INTERSTATE SYSTEM.—It is hereby declared to be essential to the national interest to provide for the early completion of the "National System of Interstate Highways", as authorized and designated in accordance with section 7 of the Federal-Aid Highway Act of 1944 (58 Stat. 838). It is the intent of the Congress that the Interstate System be completed as nearly as practicable over a thirteen-year period and that the entire System in all the States be brought to simultaneous completion. Because of its primary importance to the national defense, the name of such system is hereby changed to the "National System of Interstate and Defense Highways". Such National System of Interstate and Defense Highways is hereinafter in this Act referred to as the "Interstate System."

(b) AUTHORIZATION OF APPROPRIATIONS.—For the purpose of expediting the construction, reconstruction, or improvement, inclusive of necessary bridges and tunnels, of the interstate System, including extensions thereof through urban areas, designated in accordance with the provisions of section 7 of the Federal-Aid Highway Act of 1944 (58 Stat. 838), there is hereby authorized to be appropriated the additional sum of $1,000,000,000 for, the fiscal year ending June 30, 1957 , which sum shall be in addition to the authorization heretofore made for that year, the additional sum of $1,700,000,000 for the fiscal year ending June 30, 1958, the additional sum of $2,000,000,000 for the fiscal year ending June 30, 1959, the additional sum of $2,200,000,000 for the fiscal year ending June 30, 1960, the additional sum of $2,200,000,000 for the fiscal year ending June 30, 1961, the additional sum of $2,200,000,000 for the fiscal year ending June 30, 1962, the additional sum of $2,200,000,000 for the fiscal year ending June 30, 1963, the additional sum of $2,200,000,000 for the fiscal year ending June 30, 1964, the additional sum of $2,200,000,000 for the fiscal year ending June 30, 1965, the additional sum of $2,200,000,000 for the fiscal year ending June 30, 1966, the additional sum of $2,200,000,000 for the fiscal year ending June 30, 1967, the additional sum of $1,500,000,000 for the fiscal year ending June 30, 1968, and the additional sum of $1,025,000,000 for the fiscal year ending June 30, 1969 . . .

1. The first federal road act related to the 1956 act was passed in

    A. 1916.
    B. 1938.
    C. 1944.
    D. 1954.

2. The primary goal of this act is to

    A. educate Americans on driver's safety.
    B. help middle-class Americans afford cars.
    C. promote the building of new roadways.
    D. stimulate the automobile industry.

3. This act serves as an amendment to the

    A. Federal-Aid Road Act.
    B. Federal-Aid Highway Act.
    C. Defense Highway Program.
    D. Interstate System Program.

4. The Congress intends on constructing the Interstate System over the next

    A. ten months.
    B. two years.
    C. seven years.
    D. thirteen years.

5. This act calls for the raising of additional revenues by way of

   A. donations from charitable groups.
   B. tolls from highway users.
   C. taxes on fuel, tires, and trucks.
   D. support from automobile companies.

6. The yearly appropriations for this project between 1957 and 1969 can be characterized as being

   A. consistently $1 billion or more.
   B. consistently $1 billion or less.
   C. unspecified in the document.
   D. uncertain as of the act's passing.

7. About how much will be available for extensions of highways within urban systems in the fiscal year ending on June 30, 1958?

   A. $125 million
   B. $200 million
   C. $850 million
   D. $875 million

8. Why do you think highway construction ranked high among the nation's concerns during this time?

_____

_____

_____

_____

_____

_____

_____

_____

_____

_____

_____

_____

_____

8. How did building highways change the U.S.?

_____

_____

_____

_____

_____

_____

_____

_____

_____

_____

_____

_____

_____

_____

_____

136

EXECUTIVE ORDER 10730:
DESEGREGATION OF CENTRAL HIGH SCHOOL (1957)

On May 17, 1954, the U.S. Supreme Court ruled in Brown v. Topeka Board of Education *that segregated schools were "inherently unequal" and ordered that U.S. public schools be desegregated "with all deliberate speed." Within a week of the 1954 decision, Arkansas was one of two southern states to announce it would begin immediately to take steps to comply with the* Brown *decision. Arkansas's law school had been integrated since 1949, and seven of its eight state universities had desegregated. Blacks had been appointed to state boards and elected to local offices. It had already desegregated its public buses as well as its zoo, library, and parks system. In the summer of 1957, the city of Little Rock made plans to desegregate its public schools. Little Rock's school board had voted unanimously for a plan that started with the desegregation of the high school in 1957, followed by junior high schools the next year and elementary schools following. In September 1957, nine African-American students enrolled at Central High School in Little Rock.*

On September 2nd, the night before school was to start, Arkansas Governor Orval Faubus called out the state's National Guard to surround Little Rock Central High School and prevent any black students from entering. The governor explained that his action was taken to protect citizens and property from possible violence by protesters he claimed were headed in caravans toward Little Rock. President Eisenhower, who was vacationing in Newport, Rhode Island, arranged to meet Governor Faubus to discuss the tense situation. In their brief meeting in Newport, Eisenhower thought Faubus had agreed to enroll the African-American students, so he told Faubus that his National Guard troops could stay at Central High and enforce order. However, once back in Little Rock, Governor Faubus withdrew the National Guard.

A few days later, when nine African-American students slipped into the school to enroll, a full-scale riot erupted. The situation was quickly out of control, as Governor Faubus failed to stop the violence. Finally, Congressman Brooks Hays and Little Rock Mayor Woodrow Mann asked the federal government for help, first in the form of U.S. marshals. President Dwight D. Eisenhower, as the chief law enforcement officer of the United States, was presented with a difficult problem. He was required to uphold the Constitution and the laws, but he also wanted to avoid a bloody confrontation in Arkansas. With Executive Order 10730, the president placed the Arkansas National Guard under Federal control and sent 1,000 U.S. Army paratroopers from the 101st Airborne Division to assist them in restoring order in Little Rock.

PROVIDING ASSISTANCE FOR THE REMOVAL OF AN OBSTRUCTION OF JUSTICE WITHIN THE STATE OF ARKANSAS

WHEREAS on September 23, 1957, I issued Proclamation No. 3204 reading in part as follows:

"WHEREAS certain persons in the state of Arkansas, individually and in unlawful assemblages, combinations, and conspiracies, have wifully obstructed the enforcement of orders of the United States District Court for the Eastern District of Arkansas with respect to mat ters relating to enrollment and attendance at public schools, particularly at Central High School, located in Little Rock School District, Little Rock, Arkansas; and

"WHEREAS such wilful obstruction of justice hinders the execution of the laws of that State and of the United States, and makes it impracticable to enforce such laws by the ordinary course of judicial proceedings; and

"WHEREAS such obstruction of justice constitutes a denial of the equal protection of the laws secured by the Constitution of the United States and impedes the course of justice under those laws:

"NOW, THEREFORE, I, DWIGHT D. EISENHOWER, President of the United States, under and by virtue of the authority vested in me by the Constitution and Statutes of the United States, including Chapter 15 of Title 10 of the United States Code, particularly sections 332, 333 and 334 thereof, do command all persons engaged in such obstruction of justice to cease and desist therefrom, and to disperse forthwith;" and

WHEREAS the command contained in that Proclamation has not been obeyed and wilful obstruction of enforcement of said court orders still exists and threatens to continue:

NOW, THEREFORE, by virtue of the authority vested in me by the Constitution and Statutes of the United States, including Chapter 15 of Title 10, particularly sections 332, 333 and 334 thereof, and section 301 of Title 3 of the United States Code, It is hereby ordered as follows:

SECTION 1. I hereby authorize and direct the Secretary of Defense to order into the active military service of the United States as he may deem appropriate to carry out the purposes of this Order, any or all of the units of the National Guard of the United States and of the Air National Guard of the United States within the State of Arkansas to serve in the active military service of the United States for an indefinite period and until relieved by appropriate orders.

SEC. 2. The Secretary of Defense is authorized and directed to take all appropriate steps to enforce any orders of the United States District Court for the Eastern District of Arkansas for the removal of obstruction of justice in the State of Arkansas with respect to matters relating to enrollment and attendance at public schools in the Little Rock School District, Little Rock, Arkansas. In carrying out the provisions of this section, the Secretary of Defense is authorized to use the units, and members thereof, ordered into the active military service of the United States pursuant to Section 1 of this Order.

SEC. 3. In furtherance of the enforcement of the aforementioned orders of the United States District Court for the Eastern District of Arkansas, the Secretary of Defense is authorized to use such of the armed forces of the United States as he may deem necessary.

SEC. 4. The Secretary of Defense is authorized to delegate to the Secretary of the Army or the Secretary of the Air Force, or both, any of the authority conferred upon him by this Order.

DWIGHT D. EISENHOWER
THE WHITE HOUSE,
September 24, 1957.

1. The location which will be most immediately impacted by this order is

   A. Washington, D.C.
   B. Newport, Rhode Island.
   C. Little Rock, Arkansas.
   D. the whole of Arkansas.

2. According to the document, if the situation is not resolved, what will be authorized?

   A. impeachment of the governor
   B. a strike by Central High's teachers
   C. a Supreme Court case
   D. deployment of the National Guard

3. The immediate cause of Executive Order 10730 was

   A. failure to follow Proclamation No. 3204.
   B. sudden denial of Constitutional law.
   C. rising violence against black students.
   D. a personal threat against Eisenhower.

4. What did Eisenhower empower the Secretary of Defense to do? Do you think that power was justified in this case?

   _____

   _____

   _____

   _____

   _____

   _____

   _____

   _____

   _____

   _____

   _____

   _____

   _____

   _____

   _____

President Dwight D. Eisenhower's Farewell Address (1961)

In a speech of less than ten minutes, on January 17, 1961, President Dwight Eisenhower delivered his political farewell to the American people on national television from the Oval Office of the White House. Those who expected the military leader and hero of World War II to depart his presidency with a nostalgic, "old soldier" speech like Gen. Douglas MacArthur's, were surprised at his strong warnings about the dangers of the "military-industrial complex." As President of the United States for two terms, Eisenhower had slowed the push for increased defense spending despite pressure to build more military equipment during the Cold War's arms race. Nonetheless, the American military services and the defense industry had expanded a great deal in the 1950s. Eisenhower thought this growth was needed to counter the Soviet Union, but it confounded him. Through he did not say so explicitly, his standing as a military leader helped give him the credibility to stand up to the pressures of this new, powerful interest group. He eventually described it as a necessary evil.

The end of Eisenhower's term as president not only marked the end of the 1950s, but also the end of an era in government. A new, younger generation was rising to national power that would set a more youthful, vigorous course. His farewell address was a warning to his successors of one of the many things they would have to be wary of in the coming years.

My fellow Americans:

Three days from now, after half a century in the service of our country, I shall lay down the responsibilities of office as, in traditional and solemn ceremony, the authority of the Presidency is vested in my successor.

This evening I come to you with a message of leave-taking and farewell, and to share a few final thoughts with you, my countrymen.

Like every other citizen, I wish the new President, and all who will labor with him, Godspeed. I pray that the coming years will be blessed with peace and prosperity for all.

Our people expect their President and the Congress to find essential agreement on issues of great moment, the wise resolution of which will better shape the future of the Nation.

My own relations with the Congress, which began on a remote and tenuous basis when, long ago, a member of the Senate appointed me to West Point, have since ranged to the intimate during the war and immediate post-war period, and, finally, to the mutually interdependent during these past eight years.

In this final relationship, the Congress and the Administration have, on most vital issues, cooperated well, to serve the national good rather than mere partisanship, and so have assured that the business of the Nation should go forward. So, my official relationship with the Congress ends in a feeling, on my part, of gratitude that we have been able to do so much together.

II

We now stand ten years past the midpoint of a century that has witnessed four major wars among great nations. Three of these involved our own country. Despite these holocausts America is today the strongest, the most influential and most productive nation in the world. Understandably proud of this pre-eminence, we yet realize that America's leadership and prestige depend, not merely upon our unmatched material progress, riches and military strength, but on how we use our power in the interests of world peace and human betterment.

III

Throughout America's adventure in free government, our basic purposes have been to keep the peace; to foster progress in human achievement, and to enhance liberty, dignity and integrity among people and among nations. To strive for less would be unworthy of a free and religious people. Any failure traceable to arrogance, or our lack of comprehension or readiness to sacrifice would inflict upon us grievous hurt both at home and abroad.

Progress toward these noble goals is persistently threatened by the conflict now engulfing the world. It commands our whole attention, absorbs our very beings. We face a hostile ideology—global in scope, atheistic in character, ruthless in purpose, and insidious in method. Unhappily the danger it poses promises to be of indefinite duration. To meet it successfully, there is called for, not so much the emotional and transitory sacrifices of crisis, but rather those which enable us to carry forward steadily, surely, and without complaint the burdens of a prolonged and complex struggle—with liberty at stake. Only thus shall we remain, despite every provocation, on our charted course toward permanent peace and human betterment.

Crises there will continue to be. In meeting them, whether foreign or domestic, great or small,there is a recurring temptation to feel that some spectacular and costly action could become the miraculous solution to all current difficulties. A huge increase in newer elements of our defense; development of unrealistic programs to cure every ill in agriculture; a dramatic expansion in basic and applied research—these and many other possibilities, each possibly promising in itself, may be suggested as the only way to the road we which to travel.

But each proposal must be weighed in the light of a broader consideration: the need to maintain balance in and among national programs—balance between the private and the public economy, balance between cost and hoped for advantage—balance between the clearly necessary and the comfortably desirable; balance between our essential requirements as a nation and the duties imposed by the nation upon the individual; balance between action of the moment and the national welfare of the future. Good judgment seeks balance and progress; lack of it eventually finds imbalance and frustration.

The record of many decades stands as proof that our people and their government have, in the main, understood these truths and have responded to them well, in the face of stress and threat. But threats, new in kind or degree, constantly arise. I mention two only.

IV

A vital element in keeping the peace is our military establishment. Our arms must be mighty, ready for instant action, so that no potential aggressor may be tempted to risk his own destruction.

Our military organization today bears little relation to that known by any of my predecessors in peace time, or indeed by the fighting men of World War II or Korea.

Until the latest of our world conflicts, the United States had no armaments industry. American makers of plowshares could, with time and as required, make swords as well. But now we can no longer risk emergency improvisation of national defense; we have been compelled to create a permanent armaments industry of vast proportions. Added to this, three and a half million men and women are directly engaged in the defense establishment. We annually spend on military security more than the net income of all United State corporations.

This conjunction of an immense military establishment and a large arms industry is new in the American experience. The total influence—economic, political, even spiritual—is felt in every city, every state house, every office of the Federal government. We recognize the imperative need for this development. Yet we must not fail to comprehend its grave implications. Our toil, resources and livelihood are all involved; so is the very structure of our society.

In the councils of government, we must guard against the acquisition of unwarranted influence, whether sought or unsought, by the military-industrial complex. The potential for the disastrous rise of misplaced power exists and will persist.

We must never let the weight of this combination endanger our liberties or democratic processes. We should take nothing for granted only an alert and knowledgeable citizenry can compel the proper meshing of huge industrial and military machinery of defense with our peaceful methods and goals, so that security and liberty may prosper together.

Akin to, and largely responsible for the sweeping changes in our industrial-military posture, has been the technological revolution during recent decades.

In this revolution, research has become central; it also becomes more formalized, complex, and costly. A steadily increasing share is conducted for, by, or at the direction of, the Federal government.

Today, the solitary inventor, tinkering in his shop, has been over shadowed by task forces of scientists in laboratories and testing fields. In the same fashion, the free university, historically the fountainhead of free ideas and scientific discovery, has experienced a revolution in the conduct of research. Partly because of the huge costs involved, a government contract becomes virtually a substitute for intellectual curiosity. For every old blackboard there are now hundreds of new electronic computers.

The prospect of domination of the nation's scholars by Federal employment, project allocations, and the power of money is ever present and is gravely to be regarded.

Yet, in holding scientific research and discovery in respect, as we should, we must also be alert to the equal and opposite danger that public policy could itself become the captive of a scientific-technological elite.

It is the task of statesmanship to mold, to balance, and to integrate these and other forces, new and old, within the principles of our democratic system—ever aiming toward the supreme goals of our free society.

V

Another factor in maintaining balance involves the element of time. As we peer into society's future, we—you and I, and our government—must avoid the impulse to live only for today, plundering, for our own ease and convenience, the precious resources of tomorrow. We cannot mortgage the material assets of our grandchildren without risking the loss also of their political and spiritual heritage. We want democracy to survive for all generations to come, not to become the insolvent phantom of tomorrow.

VI

Down the long lane of the history yet to be written America knows that this world of ours, ever growing smaller, must avoid becoming a community of dreadful fear and hate, and be, instead, a proud confederation of mutual trust and respect.

Such a confederation must be one of equals. The weakest must come to the conference table with the same confidence as do we, protected as we are by our moral, economic, and military strength. That table, though scarred by many past frustrations, cannot be abandoned for the certain agony of the battlefield.

Disarmament, with mutual honor and confidence, is a continuing imperative. Together we must learn how to compose difference, not with arms, but with intellect and decent purpose. Because this need is so sharp and apparent I confess that I lay down my official responsibilities in this field with a definite sense of disappointment. As one who has witnessed the horror and the lingering sadness of war—as one who knows that another war could utterly destroy this civilization which has been so slowly and painfully built over thousands of years—I wish I could say tonight that a lasting peace is in sight.

Happily, I can say that war has been avoided. Steady progress toward our ultimate goal has been made. But, so much remains to be done. As a private citizen, I shall never cease to do what little I can to help the world advance along that road.

VII

So—in this my last good night to you as your President—I thank you for the many opportunities you have given me for public service in war and peace. I trust that in that service you find somethings worthy; as for the rest of it, I know you will find ways to improve performance in the future.

You and I—my fellow citizens—need to be strong in our faith that all nations, under God, will reach the goal of peace with justice. May we be ever unswerving in devotion to principle, confident but humble with power, diligent in pursuit of the Nation's great goals.

To all the peoples of the world, I once more give expression to America's prayerful and continuing inspiration:

We pray that peoples of all faiths, all races, all nations, may have their great human needs satisfied; that those now denied opportunity shall come to enjoy it to the full; that all who yearn for freedom may experience its spiritual blessings; that those who have freedom will understand, also, its heavy responsibilities; that all who are insensitive to the needs of others will learn charity; that the scourges of poverty, disease and ignorance will be made to disappear from the earth, and that, in the goodness of time, all peoples will come to live together in a peace guaranteed by the binding force of mutual respect and love.

1. According to President Eisenhower, until the most recent wars, America has had no

   A. standing army.
   B. National Guard.
   C. armament industry.
   D. overseas enemies.

2. Scholars and inventors are in danger of being overshadowed by the

   A. need for new weapons.
   B. skills of foreign scientists.
   C. rise of public education.
   D. power of money.

3. The nation is tempted to meet its many challenges with a belief in

   A. no opportunities for peace.
   B. some miraculous solution.
   C. the fading importance of America.
   D. the inevitability of bloodshed.

4. Eisenhower stresses the need for

   A. suspicious vigilance.
   B. lofty ambitions.
   C. enthusiasm.
   D. balance.

5. All government officials must guard against the influence of

   A. the military-industrial complex.
   B. the checks and balances system.
   C. anti-war activism.
   D. peacetime demilitarization.

6. Eisenhower characterizes America's greatest opponent as all of the following **except**

   A. global.
   B. unbeatable.
   C. atheistic.
   D. insidious.

7. Security and liberty must prosper together due to balance between

   A. military machinery and peaceful goals.
   B. wars overseas and peace domestically.
   C. America's workers and thinkers.
   D. America's soldiers and politicians.

8. Eisenhower feels that disarmament is

   A. impossible.
   B. imperative.
   C. easily achieved.
   D. happening quickly.

9. How long does Eisenhower believe that America will face danger, and how does he recommend Americans deal with it? Do you agree with his evaluation?

_____

_____

_____

_____

_____

_____

_____

_____

_____

_____

10. Eisenhower warned against mortgaging the future of our grandchildren. What did he mean? Is this still a danger?

_____

_____

_____

_____

_____

_____

_____

_____

_____

_____

President John F. Kennedy's Inaugural Address (1961)

The inaugural ceremony is a defining moment in a president's career. No one knew this better than John F. Kennedy as he prepared for his own inauguration on January 20, 1961. He wanted his address to be short and clear. It was to be devoid of any partisan rhetoric and focused on foreign policy. He began constructing the speech in late November, working with friends and advisers. While his colleagues submitted ideas, the speech was distinctly the work of Kennedy himself. Aides recount that every sentence was worked, reworked, and reduced. It was a meticulously crafted piece of oratory that dramatically announced a generational change in the White House and called on the nation to combat "tyranny, poverty, disease, and war itself."

The climax of the speech and its most memorable phrase, "Ask not what you country can do for you—ask what you can do for your country," was honed down from a thought about sacrifice that Kennedy had long held in his mind and had expressed in various ways in campaign speeches.

Vice President Johnson, Mr. Speaker, Mr. Chief Justice, President Eisenhower, Vice President Nixon, President Truman, Reverend Clergy, fellow citizens:

We observe today not a victory of party but a celebration of freedom—symbolizing an end as well as a beginning—signifying renewal as well as change. For I have sworn before you and Almighty God the same solemn oath our forbears prescribed nearly a century and three-quarters ago.

The world is very different now. For man holds in his mortal hands the power to abolish all forms of human poverty and all forms of human life. And yet the same revolutionary beliefs for which our forebears fought are still at issue around the globe—the belief that the rights of man come not from the generosity of the state but from the hand of God.

We dare not forget today that we are the heirs of that first revolution. Let the word go forth from this time and place, to friend and foe alike, that the torch has been passed to a new generation of Americans—born in this century, tempered by war, disciplined by a hard and bitter peace, proud of our ancient heritage—and unwilling to witness or permit the slow undoing of those human rights to which this nation has always been committed, and to which we are committed today at home and around the world.

Let every nation know, whether it wishes us well or ill, that we shall pay any price, bear any burden, meet any hardship, support any friend, oppose any foe to assure the survival and the success of liberty.

This much we pledge—and more.

To those old allies whose cultural and spiritual origins we share, we pledge the loyalty of faithful friends. United there is little we cannot do in a host of cooperative ventures. Divided there is little we can do—for we dare not meet a powerful challenge at odds and split asunder.

To those new states whom we welcome to the ranks of the free, we pledge our word that one form of colonial control shall not have passed away merely to be replaced by a far more iron tyranny. We shall not always expect to find them supporting our view. But we shall always hope to find them strongly supporting their own freedom—and to remember that, in the past, those who foolishly sought power by riding the back of the tiger ended up inside.

To those people in the huts and villages of half the globe struggling to break the bonds of mass misery, we pledge our best efforts to help them help themselves, for whatever period is required—not because the communists may be doing it, not because we seek their votes, but because it is right. If a free society cannot help the many who are poor, it cannot save the few who are rich.

To our sister republics south of our border, we offer a special pledge—to convert our good words into good deeds—in a new alliance for progress—to assist free men and free governments in casting off the chains of poverty. But this peaceful revolution of hope cannot become the prey of hostile powers. Let all our neighbors know that we shall join with them to oppose aggression or subversion anywhere in the Americas. And let every other power know that this Hemisphere intends to remain the master of its own house.

To that world assembly of sovereign states, the United Nations, our last best hope in an age where the instruments of war have far outpaced the instruments of peace, we renew our pledge of support—to prevent it from becoming merely a forum for invective—to strengthen its shield of the new and the weak—and to enlarge the area in which its writ may run.

Finally, to those nations who would make themselves our adversary, we offer not a pledge but a request: that both sides begin anew the quest for peace, before the dark powers of destruction unleashed by science engulf all humanity in planned or accidental self-destruction.

We dare not tempt them with weakness. For only when our arms are sufficient beyond doubt can we be certain beyond doubt that they will never be employed.

But neither can two great and powerful groups of nations take comfort from our present course—both sides overburdened by the cost of modern weapons, both rightly alarmed by the steady spread of the deadly atom, yet both racing to alter that uncertain balance of terror that stays the hand of mankind's final war.

So let us begin anew—remembering on both sides that civility is not a sign of weakness, and sincerity is always subject to proof. Let us never negotiate out of fear. But let us never fear to negotiate.

Let both sides explore what problems unite us instead of belaboring those problems which divide us.

Let both sides, for the first time, formulate serious and precise proposals for the inspection and control of arms—and bring the absolute power to destroy other nations under the absolute control of all nations.

Let both sides seek to invoke the wonders of science instead of its terrors. Together let us explore the stars, conquer the deserts, eradicate disease, tap the ocean depths and encourage the arts and commerce.

Let both sides unite to heed in all corners of the earth the command of Isaiah—to "undo the heavy burdens . . . (and) let the oppressed go free."

And if a beachhead of cooperation may push back the jungle of suspicion, let both sides join in creating a new endeavor, not a new balance of power, but a new world of law, where the strong are just and the weak secure and the peace preserved.

All this will not be finished in the first one hundred days. Nor will it be finished in the first one thousand days, nor in the life of this Administration, nor even perhaps in our lifetime on this planet. But let us begin.

In your hands, my fellow citizens, more than mine, will rest the final success or failure of our course. Since this country was founded, each generation of Americans has been summoned to give testimony to its national loyalty. The graves of young Americans who answered the call to service surround the globe.

Now the trumpet summons us again—not as a call to bear arms, though arms we need—not as a call to battle, though embattled we are—but a call to bear the burden of a long twilight struggle, year in and year out, "rejoicing in hope, patient in tribulation"—a struggle against the common enemies of man: tyranny, poverty, disease and war itself.

Can we forge against these enemies a grand and global alliance, North and South, East and West, that can assure a more fruitful life for all mankind? Will you join in that historic effort?

In the long history of the world, only a few generations have been granted the role of defending freedom in its hour of maximum danger. I do not shrink from this responsibility—I welcome it. I do not believe that any of us would exchange places with any other people or any other generation. The energy, the faith, the devotion which we bring to this endeavor will light our country and all who serve it—and the glow from that fire can truly light the world.

And so, my fellow Americans: ask not what your country can do for you—ask what you can do for your country.

My fellow citizens of the world: ask not what America will do for you, but what together we can do for the freedom of man.

Finally, whether you are citizens of America or citizens of the world, ask of us here the same high standards of strength and sacrifice which we ask of you. With a good conscience our only sure reward, with history the final judge of our deeds, let us go forth to lead the land we love, asking His blessing and His help, but knowing that here on earth God's work must truly be our own.

1. President Kennedy's attitude toward the United Nations is one of

    A. support and assistance.
    B. anger and invective.
    C. suspicion and spying.
    D. concern and displeasure.

2. President Kennedy offers a new alliance with

    A. China.
    B. Africa.
    C. Western Europe.
    C. South America.

3. The final judge of an individual's deeds is

    A. national opinion.
    B. that individual.
    C. history.
    D. the world assembly.

4. America should never fear to

    A. attack.
    B. withdraw.
    C. ignore.
    D. negotiate.

5. Kennedy refers to nuclear weaponry as the

    A. "deadly atom."
    B. "coming plight."
    C. "wonder of the world."
    D. "pinnacle of science."

6. When Kennedy says "the torch has been passed" he is referring to the

    A. placing of blame on other nations.
    B. launching of American rockets into space.
    C. passing of ideals to younger Americans.
    D. delivery of atom bombs to the army.

7. America needs mass quantities of weapons for the primary purpose of

    A. frightening opponents into avoiding war.
    B. a sneak attack against the U.S.S.R.
    C. a campaign against all Communism.
    D. rallying weaker countries to join an alliance.

8. According to Kennedy, the modern world is unique because

    A. international travel is easy thanks to high-speed vehicles.
    B. education is widespread around the civilized world.
    C. people can solve their problems or destroy themselves.
    D. people are beginning to rely on machines for fighting.

9. To Kennedy, the principle most worth fighting for was

    A. religion.
    B. unity.
    C. liberty.
    D. peace.

10. Kennedy says that there is little that we can do without

    A. the help of God.
    B. negotiating.
    C. sacrifice.
    D. cooperating with old allies.

11. Whom do you think is President Kennedy's intended audience? How does he relate to his audience? Use evidence from the document to support your conclusion.

_____

_____

_____

_____

_____

_____

_____

_____

_____

_____

_____

_____

_____

_____

_____

_____

_____

_____

_____

_____

_____

_____

EXECUTIVE ORDER 10924: ESTABLISHMENT OF THE PEACE CORPS. (1961)

The founding of the Peace Corps is one of President John F. Kennedy's most enduring legacies. Yet it got its start in a fortuitous and unexpected moment. Kennedy, arriving late to speak to students at the University of Michigan on October 14, 1960, found himself thronged by a crowd of 10,000 students at 2:00 a.m. Speaking extemporaneously, the Presidential candidate challenged American youth to devote a part of their lives to living and working in Asia, Africa, and Latin America. Would students back his effort to form a Peace Corps? Their response was immediate: Within weeks, students organized a petition drive and gathered 1,000 signatures in support of the idea. Several hundred others pledged to serve. Enthusiastic letters poured into Democratic headquarters. This response was crucial to Kennedy's decision to make the founding of a Peace Corps a priority. Since then, more than 168,000 citizens of all ages and backgrounds have worked in more than 130 countries throughout the world as volunteers in such fields as health, teaching, agriculture, urban planning, skilled trades, forestry, sanitation, and technology.

By 1960, two bills were introduced in Congress that were the direct forerunners of the Peace Corps. Representative Henry S. Reuss of Wisconsin proposed that the government study the idea. Senator Hubert Humphrey of Minnesota asked for the establishment of a Peace Corps itself. These bills were not likely to pass Congress at the time, but they caught the attention of then-Senator Kennedy for several important reasons. In contrast to previous administrations, Kennedy foresaw a "New Frontier" inspired by Roosevelt's New Deal. The New Frontier envisioned programs to fight poverty, help cities, and expand governmental benefits to a wide array of Americans. In foreign affairs, Kennedy was also more of an activist than his predecessor. He viewed the presidency as "the vital center of action in our whole scheme of government." Concerned by what was then perceived to be the global threat of communism, Kennedy looked for creative as well as military solutions. He was eager to revitalize our program of economic aid and to counter negative images of the "Ugly American" and Yankee imperialism. He believed that sending idealistic Americans abroad to work at the grassroots level would spread American goodwill into the Third World and help stem the growth of communism there.

Kennedy lost no time in actualizing his dream for a Peace Corps. Between his election and inauguration, he ordered Sargent Shriver, his brother-in-law, to do a feasibility study. Shriver remembered, "We received more letters from people offering to work in or to volunteer for the Peace Corps, which did not then exist, than for all other existing agencies." Within two months of taking office, Kennedy issued an Executive order establishing the Peace Corps within the State Department, using funds from mutual security appropriations. Shriver, as head of the new agency, assured its success by his fervent idealism and his willingness to improvise and take action. But to have permanency and eventual autonomy, the Peace Corps would have to be approved and funded by Congress. In September 1961, the 87th Congress passed Public Law 87-293 establishing a Peace Corps. By this time, because of Kennedy's Executive order and Shriver's leadership, Peace Corps volunteers were already in the field.

ESTABLISHMENT AND ADMINISTRATION OF THE PEACE CORPS IN THE DEPARTMENT OF STATE

By virtue of the authority vested in me by the Mutual Security Act of 1954, 68 Stat. 832, as amended (22 U.S.C. 1750 et seq.), and as President of the United States, it is hereby ordered as follows:

SECTION 1. Establishment of the Peace Corps. The Secretary of State shall establish an agency in the Department of State which shall be known as the Peace Corps. The Peace Corps shall be headed by a Director.

SEC. 2. Functions of the Peace Corps. (a) The Peace Corps shall be responsible for the training and service abroad of men and women of the United States in new programs of assistance to nations and areas of the world, and in conjunction with or in support of existing economic assistance programs of the United States and of the United Nations and other international organizations.

(b) The Secretary of State shall delegate, or cause to be delegated, to the Director of the Peace Corps such of the functions under the Mutual Security Act of 1954, as amended, vested in the President and delegated to the Secretary, or vested in the Secretary, as the Secretary shall deem necessary for the accomplishment of the purposes of the Peace Corps.

SEC. 3. Financing of the Peace Corps. The Secretary of State shall provide for the financing of the Peace Corps with funds available to the Secretary for the performance of functions under the Mutual Security Act of 1954, as amended.

SEC. 4. Relation to Executive Order No. 10893. This order shall not be deemed to supersede or derogate from any provision of Executive Order No. 10893 of November 8, 1960, as amended, and any delegation made by or pursuant to this order shall, unless otherwise specifically provided therein, be deemed to be in addition to any delegation made by or pursuant to that order.

JOHN F. KENNEDY

THE WHITE HOUSE,

March 1, 1961

1. According to the document, who will finance the establishment of the Peace Corps?

    A. the President
    B. the Secretary of State
    C. the United Nations
    D. the Department of State

2. According to the document, which of the following is a function of the Peace Corps?

    A. train people living in the U.S. to assist in other countries
    B. bolster the economic opportunities in the U.S.
    C. train people living in the U.S. to teach the poor
    D. fund international organizations that help people in need

3. According to this document, who will head the Peace Corps?

    A. the Secretary of State
    B. the President
    C. a director
    D. a manager

4. Using the document and what you know about history, how does the Peace Corps help the United States and other countries in the world? Use details and information from the document to support your answer.

_____

_____

_____

_____

_____

_____

_____

_____

_____

_____

_____

_____

_____

_____

_____

_____

_____

_____

_____

_____

ENGEL V. VITALE (1962)

For many years, a particular ritual marked the beginning of each school day all across America. Teachers led their students through the Pledge of Allegiance, a short prayer, the singing of "America" or "The Star Spangled Banner," and possibly some readings from the Bible. The choice of ritual varied according to state law, local custom and the preferences of individual teachers or principals.

In New York, the state Board of Regents had prepared a "non-denominational" prayer for use in the public schools, trying to avoid anything that might offend one particular religious group or another. But in one school district a group of parents challenged the prayer as "contrary to the beliefs, religions, or religious practices of both themselves and their children." The state's highest court upheld the use of the prayer, on the grounds that state law did not force any student to join in the prayer over a parent's objections.

But the Supreme Court, in the following case, held the entire idea of a state-mandated or state-sponsored prayer, no matter how innocuous, as contrary to the spirit and command of the First Amendment's ban against the establishment of religion. As Justice Black noted, a prayer by any definition constituted a religious activity. By promoting prayer, the state violated the Establishment Clause.

The Engel *decision unleashed a firestorm of criticism against the court that, although it has abated from time to time, has never died out. There are many people in the United States who believe that religion should be fostered by the state, and that while no particular doctrine or church should be established, the state ought to be friendly and supportive to all religions on an equal basis. In their opinion, school prayer was a natural and historic tradition in a country that styled itself "one nation under God."*

The court's decision has had its champions as well. Many people believe that the court was absolutely right, and that religion is and should remain a private matter. Once a teacher starts to lead students in prayer, it is difficult for any particular student to object or to abstain, and thus he or she is forced to pray—a clear violation of the First Amendment. The debate continues. Engel—to both its detractors and supporters—is a landmark decision in the effort to define what freedom of religion means in a democratic society.

Justice Black delivered the opinion of the Court.

The respondent Board of Education of Union Free School District No. 9, New Hyde Park, New York, acting in its official capacity under state law, directed the School District's principal to cause the following prayer to be said aloud by each class in the presence of a teacher at the beginning of each school day:

Almighty God, we acknowledge our dependence upon Thee, and we beg Thy blessing upon us, our parents, our teachers and our Country.

This daily procedure was adopted on the recommendation of the State Board of Regents, a governmental agency created by the State Constitution to which the New York Legislature has granted broad supervisory, executive, and legislative powers over the State's public school system. These state officials composed the prayer which they recommended and published as a part of their "Statement on Moral and Spiritual Training in the Schools," saying: "We believe that this Statement will be subscribed to by all men and women of good will, and we call upon all of them to aid in giving life to our program." . . .

We think that by using its public school system to encourage recitation of the Regents' prayer, the State of New York has adopted a practice wholly inconsistent with the Establishment Clause. There can, of course, be no doubt that New York's program of daily classroom invocation of God's blessings as prescribed in the Regents' prayer is a religious activity. It is a solemn avowal of divine faith and supplication for the blessing of the Almighty. The nature of such a prayer has always been religious, none of the respondents has denied this and the trial court expressly so found . . .

The petitioners contend among other things that the state laws requiring or permitting use of the Regents' prayer must be struck down as a violation of the Establishment Clause because that prayer was composed by governmental officials as a part of a governmental program to further religious beliefs. For this reason, petitioners argue, the State's use of the Regents' prayer in its public school system breaches the constitutional wall of separation between Church and State. We agree with that contention since we think that the constitutional prohibition against laws respecting an establishment of religion must at least mean that in this country it is no part of the business of government to compose official prayers for any group of the American people to recite as a part of a religious program carried on by government.

It is a matter of history that this very practice of establishing governmentally composed prayers for religious services was one of the reasons which caused many of our early colonists to leave England and seek religious freedom in America. The Book of Common Prayer, which was created under governmental direction and which was approved by Acts of Parliament in 1548 and 1549, set out in minute detail the accepted form and content of prayer and other religious ceremonies to be used in the established, tax-supported Church of England . . .

1. The school prayer in question was to be recited each morning by

    A. all students.
    B. willing students.
    C. religion teachers.
    D. the principal.

2. In instituting the prayer, the Board of Education was acting under

    A. institutional law.
    B. local law.
    C. state law.
    D. federal law.

3. The State Board of Regents believed the prayer would be accepted by all

    A. Christians.
    B. religious people.
    C. young people.
    D. people of good will.

4. The court referred to the Regents' prayer as

    A. "an avowal of divine faith."
    B. "an avowal of patriotism."
    C. "a wholesome statement."
    D. "an atheistic statement."

5. How does the court draw from history in the making of their decision? Do you agree that the history they outline is relevant to the case?

_____

_____

_____

_____

_____

_____

_____

_____

_____

_____

_____

_____

_____

_____

_____

_____

_____

_____

_____

_____

Test Ban Treaty (1963)

In August 1945, when the United States dropped two atomic bombs on Japan, World War II came to a conclusion.

Continued testing of atomic and then hydrogen devices lead to a rising concern about the effects of radioactive fallout. As knowledge of the nature and effects of fallout increased, and as it became apparent that no region in the world was untouched by radioactive debris, the issue of continued nuclear tests drew widened and intensified public attention. Apprehension was expressed about the possibility of a cumulative contamination of the environment and of resultant genetic damage.

Efforts to negotiate an international agreement to end nuclear tests began in the Subcommittee of Five (the United States, the United Kingdom, Canada, France, and the Soviet Union) of the United Nations Disarmament Commission in May 1955. Public interest in the course of the negotiations was active and persistent. A dozen resolutions of the UN General Assembly addressed the issue, repeatedly urging conclusion of an agreement to ban tests under a system of international controls. Efforts to achieve a test ban agreement extended over eight years because they involved complex technical problems of verification and the difficulties of reconciling deep-seated differences in approach to arms control and security. The uneven progress of the negotiations was also a result of regular fluctuations in East–West political relationships during the Cold War.

The Test Ban Treaty was signed in Moscow on August 5, 1963; ratified by the United States Senate on September 24, 1963; and entered into force on October 11, 1963. The treaty prohibited nuclear weapons tests "or any other nuclear explosion" in the atmosphere, in outer space, and under water. While not banning tests underground, the treaty prohibited such explosions if they caused "radioactive debris to be present outside the territorial limits of the State under whose jurisdiction or control" the explosions were conducted. In accepting limitations on testing, the nuclear powers accepted as a common goal "an end to the contamination of man's environment by radioactive substances."

TREATY banning nuclear weapon tests in the atmosphere, in outer space and under water

The Governments of the United States of America, the United Kingdom of Great Britain and Northern Ireland, and the Union of Soviet Socialist Republics, hereinafter referred to as the "Original Parties,"

Proclaiming as their principal aim the speediest possible achievement of an agreement on general and complete disarmament under strict international control in accordance with the objectives of the United Nations which would put an end to the armaments race and eliminate the incentive to the production and testing of all kinds of weapons, including nuclear weapons,

Seeking to achieve the discontinuance of all test explosions of nuclear weapons for all time, determined to continue negotiations to this end, and desiring to put an end to the contamination of mans environment by radioactive substances,

Have agreed as follows:

Article I

1. Each of the Parties to this Treaty undertakes to prohibit, to prevent, and not to carry out any nuclear weapon test explosion, or any other nuclear explosion, at any place under its jurisdiction or control:

    (a) in the atmosphere; beyond its limits, including outer space; or under water, including territorial waters or high seas; or

    (b) in any other environment if such explosion causes radioactive debris to be present outside the territorial limits of the State under whose jurisdiction or control such explosion is conducted. It is understood in this connection that the provisions of this subparagraph are without prejudice to the conclusion of a Treaty resulting in the permanent banning of all nuclear test explosions, including all such explosions underground, the conclusion of which, as the Parties have stated in the Preamble to this Treaty, they seek to achieve.

2. Each of the Parties to this Treaty undertakes furthermore to refrain from causing, encouraging, or in any way participating in, the carrying out of any nuclear weapon test explosion, or any other nuclear explosion, anywhere which would take place in any of the environments described, or have the effect referred to, in paragraph 1 of this Article.

Article II

1. Any Party may propose amendments to this Treaty. The text of any proposed amendment shall be submitted to the Depositary Governments which shall circulate it to all Parties to this Treaty. Thereafter, if requested to do so by one-third or more of the Parties, the Depositary Governments shall convene a conference, to which they shall invite all the Parties, to consider such amendment.

2. Any amendment to this Treaty must be approved by a majority of the votes of all the Parties to this Treaty, including the votes of all of the Original Parties. The amendment shall enter into force for all Parties upon the deposit of instruments of ratification by a majority of all the Parties, including the instruments of ratification of all of the Original Parties.

Article III

1. This Treaty shall be open to all States for signature. Any State which does not sign this Treaty before its entry into force in accordance with paragraph 3 of this Article may accede to it at any time.

2. This Treaty shall be subject to ratification by signatory States. Instruments of ratification and instruments of accession shall be deposited with the Governments of the Original Parties—the United States of America, the United Kingdom of Great Britain and Northern Ireland, and the Union of Soviet Socialist Republics—which are hereby designated the Depositary Governments.

3. This Treaty shall enter into force after its ratification by all the Original Parties and the deposit of their instruments of ratification.

4. For States whose instruments of ratification or accession are deposited subsequent to the entry into force of this Treaty, it shall enter into force on the date of the deposit of their instruments of ratification or accession.

5. The Depositary Governments shall promptly inform all signatory and acceding States of the date of each signature, the date of deposit of each instrument of ratification of and accession to this Treaty, the date of its entry into force, and the date of receipt of any requests for conferences or other notices.

6. This Treaty shall be registered by the Depositary Governments pursuant to Article 102 of the Charter of the United Nations.

Article IV

This Treaty shall be of unlimited duration.

Each Party shall in exercising its national sovereignty have the right to withdraw from the Treaty if it decides that extraordinary events, related to the subject matter of this Treaty, have jeopardized the supreme interests of its country. It shall give notice of such withdrawal to all other Parties to the Treaty three months in advance.

Article V

This Treaty, of which the English and Russian texts are equally authentic, shall be deposited in the archives of the Depositary Governments. Duly certified copies of this Treaty shall be transmitted by the Depositary Governments to the Governments of the signatory and acceding States.

IN WITNESS WHEREOF the undersigned, duly authorized, have signed this Treaty.

DONE in triplicate at the city of Moscow the fifth day of August, one thousand nine hundred and sixty-three.

For the Government of the United States of America
DEAN RUSK

For the Government of the United Kingdom of Great Britain and Northern Ireland
SIR DOUGLAS HOME

For the Government of the Union of Soviet Socialist Republics
A. GROMYKO

1. How long will this treaty be in force?

    A. until it is amended
    B. five years
    C. ten years
    D. indefinitely

2. In order for this treaty to be amended, the proposed amendment must be approved by

    A. all of the Original Parties.
    B. a majority of the Original Parties.
    C. all of the Parties.
    D. two of the Original Parties.

3. Which of the following was **not** referred to as being one of the Original Parties?

   A. Great Britain
   B. Northern Ireland
   C. United States
   D. Japan

4. Which of the following would **not** be allowed under the Test Ban Treaty?

   A. firing a weapon in a public place
   B. emitting smoke into the air
   C. testing a radioactive substance in space
   D. dumping chemicals into water

5. Do you think countries should have the right to test nuclear weapons? Use details from the document to support your answer.

_____

_____

_____

_____

_____

_____

_____

_____

_____

_____

_____

_____

_____

_____

_____

_____

_____

_____

_____

160

GIDEON V. WAINWRIGHT (1963)

Winston Churchill once said that the true measure of a civilized society is how it treats people accused of crimes. Although the Bill of Rights included a number of protections for people accused of crime, many of these guarantees went unenforced in state courts, which were held to be outside the reach of the federal Bill of Rights. This policy began to change in the 1930s, and during the 1960s was transformed with almost breathtaking speed by the Supreme Court headed by Earl Warren.

The American right to have assistance of counsel in all criminal cases marked a significant departure from the earlier English practice, which allowed lawyers only in some misdemeanor cases. In ordinary felony cases Great Britain did not permit counsel at all until 1836, although judges evidently often bent this rule. Twelve of the original thirteen states rejected the English doctrine, and extended the right to have counsel to all criminal cases. Although the Sixth Amendment, which guarantees the right to counsel, makes no reference to providing lawyers for poor people, the federal government began the practice of appointing lawyers in serious cases in the nineteenth century, and a number of states also provided counsel for indigents in felony trials in the twentieth century.

In 1932, in a famous case entitled Powell v. Alabama *(involving the Scottsboro boys), the court had held that the right to a lawyer was an essential safeguard of liberty, but it left it to the states to determine just how far this right extended. In* Betts v. Brady *(1942), the justices ruled that whether a lawyer was required would depend upon the circumstances in each case. In some circumstances, the court held a lawyer was essential to a fair trial; in others a lawyer might not be needed.*

For the next twenty years, the court heard many cases, and in nearly all of them ruled that a lawyer was in fact necessary. By the early 1960s, a majority of the court felt the time had come to jettison the Betts rule and extend the Sixth Amendment right to counsel to all persons accused of crime. That ruling came in Gideon v. Wainwright.

The whole rationale behind this and other court rulings in the 1960s was the belief that the exercise of constitutional rights ought not to depend on a person's wealth or education. In terms of this section, the court opened up the criminal justice system, made it more democratic, and permitted even people accused of crimes, perhaps the most despised group in a society, to share fully in what the Constitution promised to all Americans, basic liberties to ensure that they received a fair trial.

Justice Black delivered the opinion of the Court.

Petitioner was charged in a Florida state court with having broken and entered a poolroom with intent to commit a misdemeanor. This offense is a felony under Florida law. Appearing in court without funds and without a lawyer, petitioner asked the court to appoint counsel for him, whereupon the following colloquy took place:

The Court: Mr. Gideon, I am sorry, but I cannot appoint Counsel to represent you in this case. Under the laws of the State of Florida, the only time the Court can appoint Counsel to represent a Defendant is when that person is charged with a capital offense. I am sorry, but I will have to deny your request to appoint Counsel to defend you in this case.

The Defendant: The United States Supreme Court says I am entitled to be represented by Counsel.

Put to trial before a jury, Gideon conducted his defense about as well as could be expected from a layman. He made an opening statement to the jury, cross-examined the State's witnesses, presented witnesses in his own defense, declined to testify himself, and made a short argument "emphasizing his innocence to the charge contained in the information filed in this case." The jury returned a verdict of guilty, and petitioner was sentenced to serve five years in the state prison. Later, petitioner filed in the Florida Supreme Court this habeas corpus petition attacking his conviction and sentence on the ground that the trail court's refusal to appoint counsel for him denied him rights "guaranteed by the Constitution and the Bill of Rights by the United States Government." Treating the petition for habeas corpus as properly before it, the State Supreme Court, "upon consideration thereof" but without an opinion, denied all relief. Since 1942, when Betts v. Brady was decided by a divided Court, the problem of a defendant's federal constitutional right to counsel in a state court has been a continuing source of controversy and litigation in both state and federal courts. To give this problem another review here, we granted certiorari. . . .

The Sixth Amendment provides, "In all criminal prosecutions, the accused shall enjoy the right . . . to have the Assistance of Counsel for his defense." We have construed this to mean that in federal courts counsel must be provided for defendants unable to employ counsel unless the right is competently and intelligently waived. Betts argued that this right is extended to indigent defendants in state courts by the Fourteenth Amendment. In response the Court stated that, while the Sixth Amendment laid down "no rule for the conduct of the States, the question recurs whether the constraint laid by the Amendment upon the national courts expresses a rule so fundamental and essential to a fair trial, and so, to due process of law, that it is made obligatory upon the States by the Fourteenth Amendment." In order to decide whether the Sixth Amendment's guarantee of counsel is of this fundamental nature, the Court in Betts set out and considered "relevant data on the subject . . . afforded by constitutional and statutory provisions subsisting in the colonies and the States prior to the inclusion of the Bill of Rights in the national Constitution, and in the constitutional, legislative, and judicial history of the States to the present date." On the basis of this historical data the Court concluded that "appointment of the counsel is not a fundamental right, essential to a fair trial." It was for this reason the Betts Court refused to accept the contention that the Sixth Amendment's guarantee of counsel for indigent federal defendants was extended to or, in the words of that Court, "made obligatory upon the States by the Fourteenth Amendment." Plainly, had the Court concluded that appointment of counsel for an indigent criminal defendant was "a fundamental right, essential to a fair trial," it would have held that the Fourteenth Amendment requires appointment of counsel in a state court, just as the Sixth Amendment requires in a federal court. . . .

We accept *Betts* v. *Brady*'s assumption, based as it was on our prior cases, that a provision of the Bill of Rights which is "fundamental and essential to a fair trial" is made obligatory upon the States by the Fourteenth Amendment. We think the Court in Betts was wrong, however, in concluding that the Sixth Amendment's guarantee of counsel is not one of these fundamental rights.

. . . Florida, supported by two other States, has asked that *Betts* v. *Brady* be left intact. Twenty-two States, as friends of the Court, argue that Betts was "an anachronism when handed down" and that it should now be overruled. We agree.

The judgment is reversed and the case is remanded to the Supreme Court of Florida for further action not inconsistent with this opinion.

1. What was Gideon's alleged felony?

   A. stealing from a poolroom
   B. breaking and entering with intent to steal
   C. representing himself
   D. filing a *habeas corpus* petition

2. According to the document, which amendment requires defendants to be appointed counsel in federal courts?

   A. First Amendment
   B. Fourth Amendment
   C. Sixth Amendment
   D. Fourteenth Amendment

3. Why wasn't Gideon appointed counsel?

   A. His crime was not a capital offense.
   B. The court could not find Counsel.
   C. He preferred to represent himself.
   D. He did not have funds to hire counsel.

4. Based on this document and what you know about the law, do you think the appointment of counsel changed the outcome of many cases? Is this is a good thing? Use details from this document to support your answer.

   _____

   _____

   _____

   _____

   _____

   _____

   _____

   _____

   _____

   _____

   _____

   _____

   _____

CIVIL RIGHTS ACT (1964)

In a nationally televised address on June 6, 1963, President John F. Kennedy urged the nation to take action toward guaranteeing equal treatment of every American regardless of race. Soon after, Kennedy proposed that Congress consider civil rights legislation that would address voting rights, public accommodations, school desegregation, nondiscrimination in federally assisted programs, and more.

The assassination of John Kennedy in November 1963 left most civil rights leaders griefstricken. Kennedy had been the first president since Harry Truman to champion equal rights for black Americans, and they knew little about his successor, Lyndon Baines Johnson. Although Johnson had helped engineer the Civil Rights Act of 1957, that had been a mild measure. No one knew if the Texan would continue Kennedy's call for civil rights or move to placate his fellow southerners.

But on November 27, 1963, addressing the Congress and the nation for the first time as president, Johnson called for passage of the civil rights bill as a monument to the fallen Kennedy. "Let us continue," he declared, promising that "the ideas and the ideals which [Kennedy] so nobly represented must and will be translated into effective action." Moreover, where Kennedy had been sound on principle, Lyndon Johnson was the master of parliamentary procedure. He used his considerable talents as well as the prestige of the presidency in support of the bill.

On February 10, 1964, the House of Representatives passed the measure by a lopsided 290–130 vote, but everyone knew that the real battle would be in the Senate, whose rules had allowed southerners in the past to mount filibusters that had effectively killed nearly all civil rights legislation. But Johnson pulled every string he knew, and had the civil rights leaders mount a massive lobbying campaign, including inundating the Capitol with religious leaders of all faiths and colors. The strategy paid off. In June, the Senate voted to close debate. A few weeks later, it passed the most important piece of civil rights legislation in the nation's history. On July 2, 1964, President Johnson signed it into law.

Some members of Congress, however, worried whether the law would pass constitutional muster, since in 1883 the Supreme Court had voided the last civil rights measure, declaring such action beyond the scope of congressional power. They need not have worried this time. The Supreme Court accepted two cases on an accelerated basis and in both of them the court unanimously upheld the power of Congress under the Fourteenth Amendment to protect the civil rights of black Americans.

An Act

To enforce the constitutional right to vote, to confer jurisdiction upon the district courts of the United States to provide injunctive relief against discrimination in public accommodations, to authorize the Attorney General to institute suits to protect constitutional rights in public facilities and public education, to extend the Commission on Civil Rights, to prevent discrimination in federally assisted programs, to establish a Commission on Equal Employment Opportunity, and for other purposes.

Be it enacted by the Senate and House of Representatives of the United States of America in Congress assembled, That this Act may be cited as the "Civil Rights Act of 1964."

... TITLE VII—EQUAL EMPLOYMENT OPPORTUNITY

... DISCRIMINATION BECAUSE OF RACE, COLOR, RELIGION, SEX, OR NATIONAL ORIGIN

SEC. 703. (a) It shall be an unlawful employment practice for an employer—

(1) to fail or refuse to hire or to discharge any individual, or otherwise to discriminate against any individual with respect to his compensation, terms, conditions, or privileges of employment, because of such individual's race, color, religion, sex, or national origin; or

(2) to limit, segregate, or classify his employees in any way which would deprive or tend to deprive any individual of employment opportunities or otherwise adversely affect his status as an employee, because of such individual's race, color, religion, sex, or national origin.

(b) It shall be an unlawful employment practice for an employment agency to fail or refuse to refer for employment, or otherwise to discriminate against, any individual because of his race, color, religion, sex, or national origin, or to classify or refer for employment any individual on the basis of his race, color, religion, sex, or national origin.

(c) It shall be an unlawful employment practice for a labor organization—

(1) to exclude or to expel from its membership, or otherwise to discriminate against, any individual because of his race, color, religion, sex, or national origin;

(2) to limit, segregate, or classify its membership, or to classify or fail or refuse to refer for employment any individual, in any way which would deprive or tend to deprive any individual of employment opportunities, or would limit such employment opportunities or otherwise adversely affect his status as an employee or as an applicant for employment, because of such individual's race, color, religion, sex, or national origin; or

(3) to cause or attempt to cause an employer to discriminate against an individual in violation of this section.

(d) It shall be an unlawful employment practice for any employer, labor organization, or joint labor-management committee controlling apprenticeship or other training or retraining, including on-the-job training programs to discriminate against any individual because of his race, color, religion, sex, or national origin in admission to, or employment in, any program established to provide apprenticeship or other training.

1. Section VII deals with

   A. voting rights.
   B. housing.
   C. access to public facilities.
   D. employment.

2. The Civil Rights Act protects people from discrimination for all of the following **except**

   A. race.
   B. sex.
   C. age.
   D. religion.

3. Discuss what the document says about discrimination regarding apprentices or those in training. Use details from the document to support your answer.

_____

_____

_____

_____

_____

_____

_____

_____

_____

_____

_____

_____

_____

_____

_____

_____

_____

_____

_____

_____

_____

_____

_____

4. Do you think it is a violation of the Civil Rights Act of 1964 for women to be paid less than a man would be for doing a certain job? Why or why not?

_____

_____

_____

_____

_____

_____

_____

_____

_____

_____

_____

_____

_____

_____

_____

_____

_____

_____

_____

_____

_____

_____

_____

_____

_____

Tonkin Gulf Resolution (1964)

On August 4, 1964, President Lyndon Johnson announced that two days earlier, U.S. ships in the Gulf of Tonkin had been attacked by the North Vietnamese. Johnson dispatched U.S. planes against the attackers and asked Congress to pass a resolution to support his actions. The joint resolution "to promote the maintenance of international peace and security in southeast Asia" passed on August 7, with only two Senators (Wayne Morse and Ernest Gruening) dissenting. It became the subject of great political controversy in the course of the undeclared war that followed.

As a result, President Johnson, and later President Nixon, relied on the resolution as the legal basis for their military policies in Vietnam.

As public resistance to the war heightened, the resolution was repealed by Congress in January 1971.

Eighty-eighth Congress of the United States of America

AT THE SECOND SESSION

Begun and held at the City of Washington on Tuesday, the seventh day of January, one thousand nine hundred and sixty-four

Joint Resolution

To promote the maintenance of international peace and security in southeast Asia.

Whereas naval units of the Communist regime in Vietnam, in violation of the principles of the Charter of the United Nations and of international law, have deliberately and repeatedly attacked United Stated naval vessels lawfully present in international waters, and have thereby created a serious threat to international peace; and

Whereas these attackers are part of deliberate and systematic campaign of aggression that the Communist regime in North Vietnam has been waging against its neighbors and the nations joined with them in the collective defense of their freedom; and

Whereas the United States is assisting the peoples of southeast Asia to protest their freedom and has no territorial, military or political ambitions in that area, but desires only that these people should be left in peace to work out their destinies in their own way: Now, therefore be it

Resolved by the Senate and House of Representatives of the United States of America in Congress assembled, That the Congress approves and supports the determination of the President, as Commander in Chief, to take all necessary measures to repel any armed attack against the forces of the United States and to prevent further aggression.

Section 2. The United States regards as vital to its national interest and to world peace the maintenance of international peace and security in southeast Asia. Consonant with the Constitution of the United States and the Charter of the United Nations and in accordance with its obligations under the Southeast Asia Collective Defense Treaty, the United States is, therefore, prepared, as the President determines, to take all necessary steps, including the use of armed force, to assist any member or protocol state of the Southeast Asia Collective Defense Treaty requesting assistance in defense of its freedom.

Section 3. This resolution shall expire when the President shall determine that the peace and security of the area is reasonably assured by international conditions created by action of the United Nations or otherwise, except that it may be terminated earlier by concurrent resolution of the Congress.

1. What is the alleged purpose of the Tonkin Gulf Resolution?

    A. to protect America's economy
    B. to suppress the Communist regime
    C. to inform Americans overseas of danger
    D. to maintain international peace

2. According to the document, those attacking U.S. naval vessels were from

    A. NortheastAsia.
    B. South Vietnam.
    C. North Vietnam.
    D. China.

3. According to the document, the United States has a right to use armed force in Southeast Asia under all of the following except the

    A. U.S. Constitution.
    B. United Nations Order of Defense.
    C. Charter of the United Nations.
    D. Southeast Asia Collective Defense Treaty.

4. What was the alleged basis for the Tokin Gulf Resolution?

    A. a local uprising by Communist forces in South Vietnam
    B. an invasion by Communist forces of North Vietnam into South Vietnam
    C. an attack on U.S. naval forces
    D. a desire to overthrow the Communist government of North Vietnam

5. Do you think the United States naval vessels had the right to be in international waters in Southeast Asia? Use details and information from the document to support your answer.

_____

_____

_____

_____

_____

_____

_____

_____

_____

_____

_____

_____

_____

_____

_____

_____

_____

_____

_____

_____

_____

_____

_____

_____

_____

_____

_____

170

VOTING RIGHTS ACT (1965)

This "act to enforce the fifteenth amendment to the Constitution" was signed into law 95 years after the amendment was ratified. In those years, African Americans in the South faced tremendous obstacles to voting, including poll taxes, literacy tests, and other bureaucratic restrictions to deny them the right to vote. They also risked harassment, intimidation, economic reprisals, and physical violence when they tried to register or vote. As a result, very few African Americans were registered voters. They had very little, if any, political power, either locally or nationally.

In 1964, numerous demonstrations were held. The considerable violence that erupted brought renewed attention to the issue of voting rights. The murder of voting-rights activists in Mississippi and the attack by state troopers on peaceful marchers in Selma, Alabama, gained national attention and persuaded President Johnson and Congress to initiate meaningful and effective national voting rights legislation. The combination of public revulsion to the violence and Johnson's political skills stimulated Congress to pass the voting rights bill on August 5, 1965.

The legislation, which President Johnson signed into law the next day, outlawed literacy tests and provided for the appointment of federal examiners (with the power to register qualified citizens to vote) in those jurisdictions that were "covered" according to a formula provided in the statute. In addition, Section 5 of the act required covered jurisdictions to obtain "preclearance" from either the District Court for the District of Columbia or the U.S. Attorney General for any new voting practices and procedures. Section 2, which closely followed the language of the 15th amendment, applied a nationwide prohibition of the denial or abridgment of the right to vote on account of race or color. The use of poll taxes in national elections had been abolished by the 24th amendment (1964) to the Constitution; the Voting Rights Act directed the Attorney General to challenge the use of poll taxes in state and local elections. In Harper v. Virginia State Board of Elections, 383 U.S. 663 (1966), *the Supreme Court held Virginia's poll tax to be unconstitutional under the 14th amendment.*

Because the Voting Rights Act of 1965 was the most significant statutory change in the relationship between the federal and state governments in the area of voting since the Reconstruction period following the Civil War, it was immediately challenged in the courts. Between 1965 and 1969, the Supreme Court issued several key decisions upholding the constitutionality of Section 5 and affirming the broad range of voting practices for which preclearance was required.

The law had an immediate impact. By the end of 1965, a quarter of a million new black voters had been registered, one-third by federal examiners. By the end of 1966, only 4 out of the 13 southern states had fewer than 50 percent of African Americans registered to vote. The Voting Rights Act of 1965 was readopted and strengthened in 1970, 1975, and 1982.

AN ACT To enforce the fifteenth amendment to the Constitution of the United States, and for other purposes.

Be it enacted by the Senate and House of Representatives of the United States of America in Congress assembled, That this Act shall be known as the "Voting Rights Act of 1965."

SEC. 2. No voting qualification or prerequisite to voting, or standard, practice, or procedure shall be imposed or applied by any State or political subdivision to deny or abridge the right of any citizen of the United States to vote on account of race or color. . . .

(1) Congress hereby declares that to secure the rights under the fourteenth amendment of persons educated in American-flag schools in which the predominant classroom language was other than English, it is necessary to prohibit the States from conditioning the right to vote of such persons on ability to read, write, understand, or interpret any matter in the English language.

(2) No person who demonstrates that he has successfully completed the sixth primary grade in a public school in, or a private school accredited by, any State or territory, the District of Columbia, or the Commonwealth of Puerto Rico in which the predominant classroom language was other than English, shall be denied the right to vote in any Federal, State, or local election because of his inability to read, write, understand, or interpret any matter in the English language, except that, in States in which State law provides that a different level of education is presumptive of literacy, he shall demonstrate that he has successfully completed an equivalent level of education in a public school in, or a private school accredited by, any State or territory, the District of Columbia, or the Commonwealth of Puerto Rico in which the predominant classroom language was other than English.

1. A citizen cannot be denied the right to vote for educational reasons as long as he or she has been educated to _____ level.

    A. a sixth-grade
    B. an eighth-grade
    C. a tenth-grade
    D. a twelfth-grade

2. This act was written primarily to enforce the

    A. fourteenth amendment of the Constitution.
    B. fifteenth amendment of the Constitution.
    C. Bill of Rights.
    D. Declaration of Independence.

3. Citizens' right to vote cannot be denied for any of the following reasons **except**

    A. race.
    B. ability to speak English.
    C. color.
    D. age.

4. Do you think it is necessary for a person to be able to read in order to vote? Why or why not? Use details and information from the document to support your answer.

_____

_____

_____

_____

_____

_____

_____

_____

_____

_____

_____

_____

_____

_____

_____

_____

_____

_____

_____

_____

_____

_____

_____

_____

NOW STATEMENT OF PURPOSE (1966)

American women in the 1960s were hardly a minority, and in fact constituted 51 percent of the population. But they began to identify with members of smaller, oppressed groups and to demand liberation and equality. Sexual discrimination was so subtle and so embedded in the fabric of American society that when the new feminists began to argue for greater equality, they triggered a great deal of hostility and anger. Yet within a fairly short time, the new women's movement had made significant strides, winning legislation that guaranteed equal pay for equal work, forbidding employment discrimination on the basis of gender and securing court victories that struck down generations-old forms of discrimination.

Undoubtedly, a key element in this awakening was the entry or return to the job market of millions of women. There they not only secured a measure of economic independence, but came face to face with deeply ingrained patterns of sexual discrimination. Women were barred—informally but nonetheless effectively—from certain types of jobs, often ones that paid better or had greater promotional opportunities. They discovered that even when they were working, society expected them also to meet certain stereotypical obligations in the home, while excusing men from sharing in childcare and household work.

A key event was the 1963 publication of Betty Friedan's The Feminine Mystique, *in which she detailed the ways society kept women in an inferior status. The book did not so much cause feminism as give voice to a movement already under way. By that time John Kennedy had already established the President's Commission on the Status of Women, and later in the year secured passage of the Equal Pay Act. In 1964, Title VII of the Civil Rights Act extended to women significant protections against discrimination.*

Against this backdrop Friedan and other feminists—including some men—joined together in 1966 to create NOW, the National Organization for Women. In the beginning, NOW directed most of its resources toward the needs of working women. It denounced the exclusion of women from professions, politics and other areas of society because of antiquated male views about women. It exposed and attacked legal and economic discrimination, such as bank practices that denied married women credit in their own names. By the end of the decade, NOW claimed more than 15,000 members.

The NOW Statement of Purpose defined the mainstream of the modern feminist movement, and even while many women—and men—decried the label, they noted that they agreed with NOW's basic demand, that women in the workforce be treated equally with men, receiving equal pay for equal work and enjoying access to jobs and promotions to which their talents entitled them.

We, men and women who hereby constitute ourselves as the National Organization for Women, believe that the time has come for a new movement toward true equality for all women in America, and toward a fully equal partnership of the sexes, as part of the world-wide revolution of human rights now taking place within and beyond our national borders.

The purpose of NOW is to take action to bring women into full participation in the mainstream of American society now, exercising all the privileges and responsibilities thereof in truly equal partnership with men.

We believe the time has come to move beyond the abstract argument, discussion and symposia over the status and special nature of women which has raged in America in recent years; the time has come to confront, with concrete action, the conditions that now prevent women from enjoying the equality of opportunity and freedom of choice which is their right as individual Americans, and as human beings.

NOW is dedicated to the proposition that women first and foremost are human beings, who, like all other people in our society, must have the chance to develop their fullest human potential. We believe that women can achieve such equality only by accepting to the full the challenges and responsibilities they share with all other people in our society, as part of the decision-making mainstream of American political, economic and social life.

We organize to initiate or support action, nationally or in any part of this nation, by individuals or organizations, to break through the silken curtain of prejudice and discrimination against women in government, industry, the professions, the churches, the political parties, the judiciary, the labor unions, in education, science, medicine, law, religion and every other field of importance in American society. . . .

There is no civil rights movement to speak for women, as there has been for Negroes and other victims of discrimination. The National Organization for Women must therefore begin to speak.

We believe that the power of American law, and the protection guaranteed by the U.S. Constitution to the civil rights of all individuals, must be effectively applied and enforced to isolate and remove patterns of sex discrimination, to ensure equality of opportunity in employment and education, and equality of civil and political rights and responsibilities on behalf of women, as well as for Negroes and other deprived groups.

We realize that women's problems are linked to many broader questions of social justice; their solution will require concerted action by many groups. Therefore, convinced that human rights for all are indivisible, we expect to give active support to the common cause of equal rights for all those who suffer discrimination and deprivation, and we call upon other organizations committed to such goals to support our efforts toward equality for women.

We do not accept the token appointment of a few women to high-level positions in government and industry as a substitute for a serious continuing effort to recruit and advance women according to their individual abilities. To this end, we urge American government and industry to mobilize the same resources of ingenuity and command with which they have solved problems of far greater difficulty than those now impeding the progress of women.

We believe that this nation has a capacity at least as great as other nations, to innovate new social institutions which will enable women to enjoy true equality of opportunity and responsibility in society, without conflict with their responsibilities as mothers and homemakers. In such innovations, America does not lead the Western world, but lags by decades behind many European countries. We do not accept the traditional assumption that a woman has to choose between marriage and motherhood, on the one hand, and serious participation in industry or the professions on the other. We question the present expectation that all normal women will retire from job or profession for ten or fifteen years, to devote their full time to raising children, only to reenter the job market at a relatively minor level. This in itself is a deterrent to the aspirations of women, to their acceptance into management or professional training courses, and to the very possibility of equality of opportunity or real choice, for all but a few women. Above all, we reject the assumption that these problems are the unique responsibility of each individual woman, rather than a basic social dilemma which society must solve. True equality of opportunity and freedom of choice for women requires such practical and possible innovations as a nationwide network of child-care centers, which will make it unnecessary for women to retire completely from society until their children are grown, and national programs to provide retraining for women who have chosen to care for their own children full time.

We believe that it is as essential for every girl to be educated to her full potential of human ability as it is for every boy—with the knowledge that such education is the key to effective participation in today's economy and that, for a girl as for a boy, education can only be serious where there is expectation that it will be used in society. We believe that American educators are capable of devising means of imparting such expectations to girl students. Moreover, we consider the decline in the proportion of women receiving higher and professional education to be evidence of discrimination. This discrimination may take the form of quotas against the admission of women to colleges and professional schools; lack of encouragement by parents, counselors and educators; denial of loans or fellowships; or the traditional or arbitrary procedures in graduate and professional training geared in terms of men, which inadvertently discriminate against women. We believe that the same serious attention must be given to high school dropouts who are girls as to boys.

We reject the current assumptions that a man must carry the sole burden of supporting himself, his wife, and family, and that a woman is automatically entitled to lifelong support by a man upon her marriage, or that marriage, home and family are primarily woman's world and responsibility—hers, to dominate, his to support. We believe that a true partnership between the sexes demands a different concept of marriage, an equitable sharing of the responsibilities of home and children and of the economic burdens of their support. We believe that proper recognition should be given to the economic and social value of homemaking and child care. To these ends, we will seek to open a reexamination of laws and mores governing marriage and divorce, for we believe that the current state of "half-equality" between the sexes discriminates against both men and women, and is the cause of much unnecessary hostility between the sexes.

We believe that women must now exercise their political rights and responsibilities as American citizens. They must refuse to be segregated on the basis of sex into separate-and-not-equal ladies' auxiliaries in the political parties, and they must demand representation according to their numbers in the regularly constituted party committees—at local, state, and national levels—and in the informal power structure, participating fully in the selection of candidates and political decision-making, and running for office themselves.

In the interests of the human dignity of women, we will protest and endeavor to change the false image of women now prevalent in the mass media, and in the texts, ceremonies, laws, and practices of our major social institutions. Such images perpetuate contempt for women by society and by women for themselves. We are similarly opposed to all policies and practices—in church, state, college, factory, or office—which, in the guise of protectiveness, not only deny opportunities but also foster in women self-denigration, dependence, and evasion of responsibility, undermine their confidence in their own abilities and foster contempt for women.

NOW will hold itself independent of any political party in order to mobilize the political power of all women and men intent on our goals. We will strive to ensure that no party, candidate, President, senator, governor, congressman, or any public official who betrays or ignores the principle of full equality between the sexes is elected or appointed to office. If it is necessary to mobilize the votes of men and women who believe in our cause, in order to win for women the final right to be fully free and equal human beings, we so commit ourselves.

We believe that women will do most to create a new image of women by acting now, and by speaking out in behalf of their own equality, freedom, and human dignity—not in pleas for special privilege, nor in enmity toward men, who are also victims of the current half-equality between the sexes—but in an active, self-respecting partnership with men. By so doing, women will develop confidence in their own ability to determine actively, in partnership with men, the conditions of their life, their choices, their future and their society.

1. NOW intends to address women's issues by way of

    A. symposia.
    B. action.
    C. argument.
    D. discussion.

2. According to the document, the first and foremost classification of women is

    A. role model.
    B. victim.
    C. mother.
    D. human being.

3. The need for an organization for women was clarified by the

    A. worsening of women's treatment.
    B. failure of previous women's organizations.
    C. rise of organizations for minority equality.
    D. modernization of the workplace.

4. NOW sees women's problems as being linked to

    A. social justice in general.
    B. foreign relations in general.
    C. the problems of men.
    D. the problems of nature.

5. By itself, the promotion of a few women to high-level positions would be considered by NOW to be

    A. token and unsatisfying.
    B. the best first step.
    C. only proper.
    D. a sign of great success.

6. In the area of women's advancement, NOW sees European countries as

    A. lagging behind most of the world.
    B. insultingly backwards.
    C. more advanced than America.
    D. just beginning to modernize.

7. Innovations that would help women include all of the following **except**

    A. educational opportunities equal to males'.
    B. emphasis on the duty of childbearing.
    C. job retraining programs for mothers.
    D. childcare centers for working mothers.

8. The primary goal of NOW is to

    A. immediately act to bring women to the mainstream.
    B. research the history of society's demands on women.
    C. inspire women to be angry at men.
    D. examine and compare the roles of men and women.

9. What is NOW's intended political stance? What is this stance meant to accomplish?

THE NEW YORK TIMES CO. V. UNITED STATES (1971)

In a democracy, there is always a tension between a free press and the government, between what the government claims ought to be kept confidential and what reporters believe the public ought to know. Rarely has this conflict been clearer than in the celebrated Pentagon Papers case.

In 1967, Secretary of Defense Robert S. McNamara ordered a full-scale evaluation of how the United States became involved in the Vietnam War. A study team of thirty-six persons took more than a year to compile the report, which ran to forty-seven volumes, with some 4,000 pages of documentary evidence and 3,000 pages of analysis. Daniel Ellsberg, a former Defense Department economist who had grown disillusioned with the war, copied major portions of the study and then turned them over to the press. On June 13, 1971, the New York Times *began publishing the papers. The Nixon administration immediately sought to stop further publication.*

In Near v. Minnesota, *Chief Justice Hughes had noted that the rule against prior restraint would not apply in certain cases. No one would question, Hughes declared, "that a government might prevent actual obstruction to its recruiting service or the publication of the sailing days of transports or the number and location of troops." Using this theory, the Justice Department secured a temporary injunction against the* Times. *The* Washington Post *then picked up publication. When the administration went to court against that paper, the* Boston Globe *began publication. In an unusual move, the Supreme Court expedited the appeals process, and heard oral argument on June 26th. Four days later, on June 30th—seventeen days after the* Times *ran the first installment—Supreme Court handed down its decision.*

The speed is noteworthy for several reasons, not least of which is the importance that both the administration and the court gave to the necessity to decide the issue. The speed also accounts, at least in part, for the failure of a majority to form around a single opinion. Instead, the court announced a brief per curiam decision, in which it noted that the government always had a heavy burden to bear in proving why prior restraint should be permitted, and it had failed to do so in this case. The various justices then set out their views of freedom of the press.

The rationale behind the pilfering of the Pentagon documents and then providing copies to the press had been to inform the public of what Ellsberg charged was double-dealing and lying by the government regarding the Vietnam War. The people, according this theory, had a right to know what its government had done. General Maxwell Taylor, who had been ambassador to South Vietnam during the early stages of the war, condemned this idea. A citizen's right to know, he declared, is limited "to those things he needs to know to be a good citizen and discharge his functions, but not to . . . secrets that damage his government and indirectly the citizen himself."

Some members of the court, notably Justice Potter Stewart, did believe in this notion of a citizen's right to know. Stewart put forward the theory of the press serving as a surrogate for the people, ferreting out information for them and securing the material to which they had a right. Not all members of the court endorsed this "functional" theory of the press, but Chief Justice Burger later commented that despite the split vote, the justices were "actually unanimous." In many ways, this was true. All of the justices did believe in the basic doctrine of no prior restraint, first set out in the Near case, and with the exception of Justices Black and Douglas, who took an absolutist stance against any government censorship of any issue at any time, the entire court agreed that no prior restraint was the rule except in very unusual circumstances.

Per Curiam.

We granted certiorari in these cases in which the United States seeks to enjoin the New York Times and the Washington Post from publishing the contents of a classified study entitled "History of U.S. Decision-Making Process on Viet Nam Policy."

"Any system of prior restraints of expression comes to this Court bearing a heavy presumption against its constitutional validity." . . . The District Court in the New York Times case and the District Court and the Court of Appeals in the Washington Post case held that the Government had not met that burden. We agree.

The judgement of the Court of Appeals for the District of Columbia Circuit is therefore affirmed. The order of the Court of Appeals for the Second Circuit is reversed and the case is remanded with directions to enter a judgement affirming the judgement of the District Court. The stays entered June 25, 1971, by the Court are vacated. The mandates shall issue forthwith.

So ordered.

Justice Black, with whom Justice Douglas joins, concurring.

> I adhere to the view that the Government's case against the Washington Post should have been dismissed and that the injunction against the New York Times should have been vacated without oral argument when the cases were first presented to this Court. I believe that every moment's continuance of the injunctions against these newspapers amounts to a flagrant, indefensible, and continuing violation of the First Amendment . . . In my view it is unfortunate that some of my Brethren are apparently willing to hold that the publication of news may sometimes be enjoined. Such a holding would make a shambles of the First Amendment . . . Only a free and unrestrained press can effectively expose deception in government. To find that the President has "inherent power" to halt the publication of news by resort to the courts would wipe out the First Amendment. The word "security" is a broad, vague generality whose contours should not be invoked to abrogate the fundamental laws embodied in the First Amendment . . .

Justice Douglas, with whom Justice Black joins, concurring.

> [The First Amendment] leaves, in my view, no room for governmental restraint on the press. There is, moreover, no statute barring the publication by the press of the material which the Times and Post seek to use . . . [I]t is apparent that Congress was capable of and did distinguish between publishing and communication in the various sections of the Espionage Act.

> So any power that the Government possesses must come from its "inherent power." The power to wage war is "the power to wage war successfully." But the war power stems from a declaration of war. The Constitution by Article I, Section 8, gives Congress, not the President, power "to declare War." Nowhere are presidential wars authorized. We need not decide therefore what leveling effect the war power of Congress might have.

> These disclosures may have a serious impact. But that is no basis for sanctioning a previous restraint on the press . . . The dominant purpose of the First Amendment was to prohibit the widespread practice of governmental suppression of embarrassing information. A debate of large proportions goes on in the Nation over our posture in Vietnam. Open debate and discussion of public issues are vital to our National Health. The stays in these cases that have been in effect for more than a week constitute a flouting of the principles of the First Amendment as interpreted in [*Near* v. *Minnesota*].

Justice Brennan, concurring.

The error that has pervaded these cases from the outset was the granting of any injunctive relief whatsoever, interim or otherwise. The entire thrust of the Government's claim throughout these cases has been that publication of the material sought to be enjoyed "could," or "might," or "may" prejudice the national interest in various ways. But the First Amendment tolerates absolutely no prior judicial restraints of the press predicated upon surmise or conjecture that untoward consequences may result. Our cases, it is true, have indicated that there is a single, extremely narrow class of cases in which the First Amendment's ban on prior judicial restraint may be overridden. Our cases have thus far indicated that such cases may arise only when the Nation "is at war" . . . during which times "no one would question but that a government might prevent actual obstruction to its recruiting service or the publication of the sailing dates of transports or the number and location of troops." . . . Even if the present world situation were assumed to be tantamount to a time of war, or if the power of presently available armaments would justify even in peacetime the suppression of information that would set in motion a nuclear holocaust, in neither of these actions has the Government presented or even alleged that publication of items from or based upon the material at issue would cause the happening of an event of that nature . . . Until the Government has clearly made out its case, the First Amendment commands that no injunction may issue.

Justice Stewart, with whom Justice White joins, concurring.

The only effective restraint upon executive policy and power in the areas of national defense and international affairs may lie in an enlightened citizenry. For this reason, it is perhaps here that a press that is alert, aware, and free most vitally serves the basic purpose of the First Amendment. Yet it is elementary that the successful conduct of international diplomacy and the maintenance of an effective national defense require both confidentiality and secrecy. I think there can be but one answer to this dilemma, if dilemma it be. The responsibility must be where the power is. The Executive must have largely unshared duty to determine and preserve the degree of internal security necessary to exercise . . . power successfully. It is the constitutional duty of the Executive—as a matter of sovereign prerogative and not as a matter of law as the courts know law—through the promulgation and enforcement of executive regulations to protect the confidentiality necessary to carry out its responsibilities in the fields of international relations and national defense. This is not to say that Congress and the courts have no role to play. Undoubtedly Congress has the power to enact specific and appropriate criminal laws to protect government property and preserve government secrets . . .

But in the cases before us we are asked neither to construe specific regulations nor to apply specific laws. We are asked, instead, to perform a function that the Constitution gave to the Executive, not the Judiciary. We are asked, quite simply, to prevent the publications by two newspapers of material that the Executive Branch insists should not, in the national interest, be published. I am convinced that the Executive is correct with respect to some of the documents involved. But I cannot say that disclosure of any of them will surely result in direct, immediate, and irreparable damage to our Nation or its people. That being so, there can under the First Amendment be but one judicial resolution of the issues before us. I join the judgements of the Court.

Justice White, with whom Justice Stewart joins, concurring.

I concur in today's judgements, but only because of the concededly extraordinary protection against prior restraints enjoyed by the press under our constitutional system. I do not say that in no circumstances would the First Amendment permit an injunction against publishing information about governent plans or operations. Nor, after examining the materials the Government characterizes as the most sensitive and destructive, can I deny that revelation of these documents will do substantial damage to public interests. Indeed, I am confident that their disclosure will have that result. But I nevertheless agree that the United States has not satisfied the very heavy burden which it must meet to warrant an injunction against publication in these cases, at least in the absence of express and appropriately limited congressional authorization for prior restraints in circumstances such as these . . .

Justice Marshall, concurring.

The ultimate issue in this case is whether this Court or the Congress has the power to make law. [I]n some situations it may be that . . . there is a basis for the invocation of the equity jurisdiction of this Court as an aid to prevent the publication of material damaging to "national security," however that term may be defined. It would, however, be utterly inconsistent with the concept of separation of powers for this Court to use its power of contempt to prevent behavior that Congress has specifically declined to prohibit. There would be similar damage to the basic concept of these co-equal branches of Government if when the [executive] had adequate authority granted by Congress to protect "national security" it can choose instead to invoke the contempt power of a court to enjoin the threatened conduct . . . It is plain that Congress has specifically refused to grant the authority the Government seeks from this Court to fling itself into every breach perceived by some Government official . . .

1. Justice Brennan believes that the publication of the information in question would

    A. significantly harm the President's reputation.
    B. not cause serious harm such as a nuclear war.
    C. cause a change in the First Amendment.
    D. not violate the First Amendment in any way.

2. Justice Douglas believes that "inherent power" applies

    A. only to the President.
    B. more to the President than Congress.
    C. more to Congress than the President.
    D. to Congress and the House of Representatives.

3. According to Justice Black, the press must have free restraint so it can

    A. report the facts accurately.
    B. expose deception in government.
    C. report facts in a timely manner.
    D. inform the public of important events.

4. Justice Stewart says that Congress has the power to enact laws to

    A. protect government property and secrets.
    B. protect the rights of the press.
    C. prevent violations to the First Amendment.
    D. prevent damage to public interests.

5. The documents that the United States did not want newspapers to publisher were about

    A. decision-making regarding the Vietnam War.
    B. measures taken to keep Americans safe during war.
    C. the President's reasons for going to war with Vietnam.
    D. how the U.S. may have violated the First Amendment.

6. Do you think the exception to the rule against prior restraint in order to prevent "obstruction of its recruiting service" would survive a challenge today if a newspaper wanted to publish a study of environmental health hazards recruits faced? Why or why not?

United States v. Nixon (1974)

In November 1972, Richard Nixon won a second term as president, decisively defeating the Democratic candidate, George McGovern. But toward the end of the campaign a group of burglars broke into the Democratic Party campaign headquarters in Washington's Watergate complex. Thanks in large part to the determined investigative reporting of the Washington Post, what had been a small news story soon expanded, as reporters uncovered tracks leading to high government officials. The Nixon administration denied any wrongdoing, but it soon became clear that it had tried to cover up the burglary and connections to it, connections that might even include the president. Under congressional and public pressure, Nixon appointed a special prosecutor. When it was learned that the president had secretly taped conversations in the Oval Office, the prosecutor filed a subpoena to secure tapes he believed relevant to the criminal investigation.

In March 1974, a federal grand jury indicted seven associates of President Nixon for conspiracy to obstruct justice and other offenses relating to the Watergate burglary. The president himself was named as an unindicted co-conspirator. The District Court, upon the motion of the special prosecutor, issued a subpoena to the president requiring him to produce certain tapes and documents relating to precisely identified meetings between the president and others. Although President Nixon released edited transcripts of some of the subpoenaed conversations, his counsel filed a "special appearance" and moved to quash the subpoena on the grounds of executive privilege. When the District Court denied the motion, the president appealed and the case was quickly brought to the Supreme Court.

In the following portion of the court's unanimous opinion, the Supreme Court dealt with two key issues, the power of the judiciary as the ultimate arbiter of the Constitution, and the claim of the president that, in the name of executive privilege, he could choose to withhold materials germane to a criminal investigation. Chief Justice Burger reaffirmed the rulings of Marbury v. Madison *and* Cooper v. Aaron *that under the Constitution the courts have the final voice in determining constitutional questions, and that no person, not even the president of the United States, is above the law.*

Although there had been some speculation as to whether Nixon would obey the court, within eight hours after the decision had been handed down the White House announced it would comply. On August 5, 1974, transcripts of sixty-four tape recordings were released, including one that was particularly damaging in regard to White House involvement in the Watergate cover-up. Three days later, his support in Congress almost completely gone, Nixon announced that he would resign.

Mr. Chief Justice Burger delivered the opinion of the Court. This litigation presents for review the denial of a motion, filed [on] behalf of the [President] in the case of United States v. Mitchell et al., to quash a third-party subpoena duces tecum . . . direct[ing] the President to produce certain tape recordings and documents relating to his conversations with aides and advisers. The court rejected the President's claims of absolute executive privilege, [and] of lack of jurisdiction . . . .

A. . . . we turn to the claim that the subpoena should be quashed because it demands "confidential conversations between a President and his close advisors that it would be inconsistent with the public interest to produce." The first contention is a broad claim that the separation of powers doctrine precludes judicial review of a President's claim of privilege. The second contention is that if he does not prevail on the claim of absolute privilege, the court should hold as a matter of constitutional law that the privilege prevails over the subpoena duces tecum.

In the performance of assigned constitutional duties each branch of the Government must initially interpret the Constitution, and the interpretation of its powers by any branch is due great respect from the other. The President's counsel [reads] the Constitution as providing an absolute privilege of confidentiality for all Presidential communications. Many decisions of this Court, however, have unequivocally reaffirmed the holding of [*Marbury* v. *Madison*] that "it is emphatically the province and duty of the judicial department to say what the law is."

No holding of the Court has defined the scope of judicial power specifically related to the enforcement of a subpoena for confidential Presidential communications for use in a criminal prosecution, but other exercises of powers by the Executive Branch and the Legislative Branch have been found invalid as in conflict with the Constitution. In a series of cases, the Court interpreted the explicit immunity conferred by express provisions of the Constitution on Members of the House and Senate by the Speech or Debate Clause. Since this Court has consistently exercised the power to construe and delineate claims arising under express powers, it must follow that the Court has authority to interpret claims with respect to powers alleged to derive from enumerated interpret claims with respect to powers.

. . . Notwithstanding the deference each branch must accord the others, the "judicial Power of the United States" vested in the federal courts by [the Constitution] can no more be shared with the Executive Branch than the Chief Executive for example, can share with the Judiciary the veto power, or the Congress share with the Judiciary the power to override a Presidential veto. Any other conclusion would be contrary to the basic concept of separation of powers and the checks and balances that flow from the scheme of a tripartite government. We therefore reaffirm that it is the province and the duty of this Court "to say what the law is" with respect to the claim of privilege presented in this case.

B. In support of his claim of absolute privilege, the President's counsel urges two grounds. The first is the valid need for protection of communications between high Government officials and those who advise and assist them in the performance of their manifold duties; the importance of this confidentiality is too plain to require further discussion. Human experience teaches that those who expect public dissemination of their remarks may well temper candor with a concern for appearances and for their own interests to the detriment of the decision-making process. Whatever the nature of the privilege of confidentiality of Presidential communications in the exercise of Art. II powers, the privilege can be said to derive from the supremacy of each branch within its own assigned areas of constitutional duties. Certain powers and privileges flow from the nature of enumerated powers; the protection of the confidentiality of Presidential communications has similar constitutional underpinnings.

The second ground asserted to support the claim of absolute privilege rests on the doctrine of separation of powers. Here it is argued that the independence of the Executive Branch within its own sphere insulates a President from a judicial subpoena in an ongoing criminal prosecution, and thereby protects confidential Presidential communications.

However, neither the doctrine of separation of powers, nor the need for confidentiality of high level communications, without more, can sustain an absolute, unqualified Presidential privilege of immunity from judicial process under all circumstances. The President's need for complete candor and objectivity from advisers calls for great deference from the court. However, when the privilege depends solely on the broad, undifferentiated claim of public interest in the confidentiality of such conversations, a confrontation with other values arises. Absent a claim of need to protect military, diplomatic, or sensitive national security secrets, we find it difficult to accept the argument that even the very important interest in confidentiality of Presidential communications is significantly diminished by production of such material for in camera inspection with all the protection that a district court will be obliged to provide.

The impediment that an absolute, unqualified privilege would place in the way of primary constitutional duty of the Judicial Branch to do justice in criminal prosecutions would plainly conflict with the function of the courts under Art. III. In designing the structure of our Government and dividing and allocating the sovereign power among three co-equal branches, the [Framers] sought to provide a comprehensive system, but the separate powers were not intended to operate with absolute independence. To read the Art. II powers of the President as providing an absolute privilege as against a subpoena essential to enforcement of criminal statutes on no more than a generalized claim of the public interest in confidentiality of nonmilitary and nondiplomatic discussions would upset the constitutional balance of "a workable government" and gravely impair the role of the courts under Art. III.

C. Since we conclude that the legitimate needs of the judicial process may outweigh Presidential privilege, it is necessary to resolve those competing interests in a manner that preserves the essential functions of each branch. The right and indeed the duty to resolve that question does not free the Judiciary from according high respect to the representations made on behalf of the President.

The expectation of a President to the confidentiality of his conversations and correspondence, like the claim of confidentiality of judicial deliberations, for example, has all the values to which we accord deference for the privacy of all citizens and added to those values the necessity for protection of the public interest in candid, objective, and even blunt or harsh opinions in Presidential decision-making. A President and those who assist him must be free to explore alternatives in the process of shaping policies and making decisions and to do so in a way many would be unwilling to express except privately. These are the considerations justifying a presumptive privilege for Presidential communications. The privilege is fundamental to the operation of government and inextricably rooted in the separation of powers under the Constitution.

. . . But this presumptive privilege must be considered in light of our historic commitment to the rule of law. This is nowhere more profoundly manifest than in our view that "the twofold aim [of criminal justice] is that guilt shall not escape or innocence suffer." . . . The need to develop all relevant facts in the adversary system is both fundamental and comprehensive. The ends of criminal justice would be defeated if judgments were to be founded on a partial or speculative presentation of the facts. . . . To ensure that justice is done, it is imperative to the function of courts that compulsory process be available for the production of evidence needed either by the prosecution or by the defense. . . . The [evidentiary] privileges are designed to protect weighty and legitimate competing interests . . . [and] are not lightly created nor expansively construed for they are in derogation of the search for truth.

In this case the President challenges a subpoena served on him as a third party requiring the production of materials for use in a criminal prosecution; he does so on the claim that he has a privilege against disclosure of confidential communications. He does not place his claim of privilege on the ground they are military or diplomatic secrets. As to these areas of Art. II duties the courts have traditionally shown the utmost deference to Presidential responsibilities. . . . No case of the Court, however, has extended this high degree of deference to a President's generalized interest in confidentiality. Nowhere in the Constitution is there any explicit reference to a privilege of confidentiality, yet to the extent this interest relates to the effective discharge of a President's powers, it is constitutionally based.

The right to the production of all evidence at a criminal trial similarly has constitutional dimensions. . . . It is the manifest duty of the courts to vindicate [the Sixth and Fifth Amendment] guarantees and to accomplish that it is essential that all relevant and admissible evidence be produced.

In this case we must weigh the importance of the general privilege of confidentiality of Presidential communications in performance of his responsibilities against inroads of such privilege on the fair administration of criminal justice. The interest in preserving confidentiality is weighty indeed and entitled to great respect. However, we cannot conclude that advisers will be moved to temper the candor of their remarks by the infrequent occasions of disclosure because of the possibility that such conversations will be called for in the context of a criminal prosecution.

On the other hand, the allowance of the privilege to withhold evidence that is demonstrably relevant in a criminal trial would cut deeply into the guarantee of due process of law and gravely impair the basic function of the courts. A President's acknowledged need for confidentiality in the communications of his office is general in nature, whereas the constitutional need for production of relevant evidence in a criminal proceeding is specific and central to the fair adjudication of a particular criminal case. Without access to specific facts a criminal prosecution may be totally frustrated. The President's broad interest in confidentiality of communications will not be vitiated by disclosure of a limited number of conversations preliminarily shown to have some bearing on the pending trials. We conclude that when the ground for asserting privilege as to subpoenaed materials sought for use in a criminal trial is based only on the generalized interests in confidentiality, it cannot prevail over the fundamental demands of due process of law in the fair administration of criminal justice. The generalized assertion of privilege must yield to the demonstrated, specific need for evidence in a pending criminal trial.

Affirmed.

1. President Nixon claimed his tapes and papers should be kept confidential using

    A. separation of powers.
    B. absolute privilege.
    C. duces tecum.
    D. *Marbury* v. *Madison*.

2. The Constitution is open for interpretation by

    A. Supreme Court justices only.
    B. the president only.
    C. all branches of government.
    D. all foreign countries.

3. Nixon believes communication with close aides must be confidential because

    A. out of all the government, he could only trust his closest personal associates.
    B. his aides would otherwise be able to inform his political enemies of his plans.
    C. he has the right to confidentiality derived from the *Marbury* v. *Madison* case.
    D. he could not communicate effectively while worried about public opinion.

4. A president would likely have the greatest opportunity to keep his documents confidential if the documents

   A. would make him unpopular.
   B. were needed in a criminal investigation.
   C. pertained to military secrets.
   D. were not kept in the White House.

5. The final ability to determine Constitutional powers usually belongs to the

   A. executive branch.
   B legislative branch.
   C. judicial branch.
   D. president.

6. How is a president's right to confidentiality different than a regular citizen's? How are their rights similar? Use evidence from the document above to support your conclusion.

_____

_____

_____

_____

_____

_____

_____

_____

_____

_____

_____

_____

_____

_____

_____

_____

_____

_____

FOREIGN AID AND HUMAN RIGHTS (1976)

The civil rights movement of the 1960s led Americans to pay greater attention to human rights outside the United States. Watchdog groups such as Amnesty International, Human Rights Watch and Trans-Africa reported on violations of basic human rights not only in openly authoritarian countries but in supposedly democratic countries as well.

At the same time, post-Vietnam criticism of American foreign policy led to a questioning of the assumption that because a country claimed to be anti-communist, it should automatically receive American support and economic aid. Instead, the argument went, foreign aid ought to be given only to democratic regimes that respected individual rights. American policy overseas, according to these critics, had only been successful in the past when it had been tied to a strong moral stance. The notion that American "interests" could lead to support of dictatorships affronted them on both a pragmatic and a moral basis.

In 1976, Congress overrode a presidential veto to enact a human rights policy into the International Security and Arms Export Control Act. While some critics claimed the provision was more symbolic than anything else, symbols do, in fact, carry great weight in shaping public perceptions. The congressional message was that as a democracy, the United States was obligated to put into practice overseas the same principles it claimed to hold dear at home, that democracy was, in fact, indivisible.

Title III—General Limitations

Human Rights

Sec. 301. (a) Section 502B of the Foreign Assistance Act of 1961 is amended to read as follows:

Sec. 502B. Human Rights.—(a) (1) It is the policy of the United States, in accordance with its international obligations as set forth in the Charter of the United Nations and in keeping with the constitutional heritage and traditions of the United States, to promote and encourage increased respect for human rights and fundamental freedoms for all without distinction as to race, sex, language, or religion. To this end, a principal goal of the foreign policy of the United States is to promote the increased observance of internationally recognized human rights by all countries.

(2) It is further the policy of the United States that, except under circumstances specified in this section, no security assistance may be provided to any country the government of which engages in a consistent pattern of gross violations of internationally recognized human rights.

(3) In furtherance of the foregoing policy the President is directed to formulate and conduct international security assistance programs of the United States in a manner which will promote and advance human rights and avoid identification of the United States, through such programs, with governments which deny to their people internationally recognized human rights and fundamental freedoms, in violation of international law or in contravention of the policy of the United States as expressed in this section or otherwise.

(b) The Secretary of State shall transmit to the Congress, as part of the presentation materials for security assistance programs proposed for each fiscal year a full and complete report, prepared with the assistance of the Coordinator for Human Rights and Humanitarian Affairs, with respect to practices regarding the observance of and respect for internationally recognized human rights in each country proposed as a recipient of security assistance. In determining whether a government falls within the provisions of subsection (a)(3) and in the preparation of any report or statement required under this section, consideration shall be given to—

(1) the relevant findings of appropriate international organizations, including nongovernmental organizations, such as the International Committee of the Red Cross; and

(2) the extent of cooperation by such government in permitting an unimpeded investigation by any such organization of alleged violations of internationally recognized human rights.

(c) (1) Upon the request of the Senate or the House of Representatives by resolution of either such House, or upon the request of the Committee on Foreign Relations of the Senate or the Committee on International Relations of the House of Representatives, the Secretary of State shall, within thirty days after receipt of such request, transmit to both such committees a statement, prepared with the assistance of the Coordinator for Human Rights and Humanitarian Affairs, with respect to the country designated in such request, setting forth—

(A) all the available information about observance of and respect for human rights and fundamental freedom in that country, and a detailed description of practices by the recipient government with respect thereto;

(B) the steps the United States has taken to—

(i) promote respect for and observance of human rights in that country and discourage any practices which are inimical to internationally recognized human rights, and

(ii) publicly or privately call attention to, and disassociate the United States and any security assistance provided for such country from, such practices;

(C) whether, in the opinion of the Secretary of State, notwithstanding any such practices—

(i) extraordinary circumstances exist which necessitate a continuation of security assistance for such country, and, if so, a description of such circumstances and the extent to which such assistance should be continued (subject to such conditions as Congress may impose under this section), and

(ii) on all the facts it is in the national interest of the United States to provide such assistance; and

(D) such other information as such committee or such House may request.

1. Which of the following is **not** a consideration in determining whether a government is violating human rights?

   A. the findings of the International Committee of the Red Cross
   B. the extent to which a government is permitting an investigation
   C. the findings of nongovernmental organizations
   D. the number of people affected by the violation

2. According to the document, the United States will **not** provide security assistance to countries

   A. that are not democracies.
   B. where the people are not free.
   C. with gross human right violations.
   D. with any human right violations.

3. According to the document, how many days does the Secretary of State have to prepare a report of a human rights investigation for a country?

   A. ten days
   B. twenty days
   C. thirty days
   D. sixty days

4. Who may assist the Secretary of State in compiling a report?

   A. the president
   B. the Red Cross
   C. Congress and the House of Representatives
   D. Coordinator for Human Rights and Humanitarian Affairs

5. Do you think the United States should have the right to refuse to provide security for a country violating its citizens' human rights. Why or why not? Use details and information from the document to support your answer.

_____

_____

_____

_____

_____

_____

_____

_____

_____

_____

_____

_____

191

Sanctions Against South Africa (1986)

Dutch settlers, known as Boers, arrived in southern Africa in the seventeenth century. The British arrived two hundred years later. At the beginning of the twentieth century, the British conquered the Dutch. The four colonies of Transvaal, the Orange Free State, Cape Colony and Natal became the Union of South Africa in 1910.

By then, all the black Africans in the area had come under white rule. They faced the usual restrictions imposed by imperial powers on native peoples. But a specific policy of racial separation, known as apartheid, did not begin until 1948, when the Afrikaners took power under D.F. Malan. In the ensuing years the government passed a number of laws that required blacks to live in designated areas and carry identification papers, and which denied them basic civil liberties and rights.

The United States, like most of the European countries, had paid little attention to apartheid at the time of its inception; moreover. Its underlying philosophy was similar to the segregation imposed by law in the southern states. With the rise of the civil rights movement in the United States and the revolt against colonial rule in Asia and Africa, voices were raised within the United States and in the United Nations against apartheid.

Within South Africa the African National Congress, headed by Nelson Mandela, led the opposition to the government's racial policies. Many of the ANC leaders, including Mandela, spent many years in jail.

In the 1970s the South African government began easing some of its racial restrictions, but the pace did not satisfy the ANC. Wide-scale violence committed by extremists on both sides took hundreds of lives. Even though the government of P.W. Botha seemed committed to ending apartheid, opponents of the system demanded more reforms and at a faster pace.

The charismatic Anglican bishop, Desmond Tutu, rallied western support with his call for a boycott of South Africa, primarily through economic sanctions. The administration of Ronald Reagan opposed formal sanctions, preferring to exert quiet pressure to speed up reform. But the demand for sanctions could not be quieted. In 1986 Congress overrode a presidential veto to ban the importation of South African goods and prohibit American business investments in South Africa.

While some critics believe the sanctions were more symbolic than anything else, others claim that they did contribute to rapid political change in South Africa. In 1990, President F.W. de Klerk released Nelson Mandela after twenty-seven years of imprisonment, opened negotiations with the ANC and scrapped most of the apartheid laws. In 1992, a strong majority of the country's white population voted to endorse de Klerk's dismantling of apartheid and the extension of political rights to the black majority. When this happened, President Bush lifted the economic sanctions, claiming that the purpose of the bill had been successfully carried out.

Title I—Policy of the United States with Respect to Ending Apartheid

Policy Toward the Government of South Africa

Sec. 101. (a) United States policy toward the Government of South Africa shall be designed to bring about reforms in that system of government that will lead to the establishment of a nonracial democracy.

(b) The United States will work toward this goal by encouraging the Government of South Africa to—

(1) repeal the present state of emergency and respect the principle of equal justice under law for citizens of all races;

(2) release Nelson Mandela, Govan Mbeki, Walter Sisulu, black trade union leaders, and all political prisoners;

(3) permit the free exercise by South Africans of all races of the right to form political parties, express political opinions, and otherwise participate in the political process;

(4) establish a timetable for the elimination of apartheid laws;

(5) negotiate with representatives of all racial groups in South Africa the future political system in South Africa, and

(6) end military and paramilitary activities aimed at neighboring states.

(c) The United States will encourage the actions set forth in subsection (b) through economic, political, and diplomatic measures as set forth in this Act. The United States will adjust its actions toward the Government of South Africa to reflect the progress or lack of progress made by the Government of South Africa in meeting the goal set forth in subsection (a).

Policy Toward the African National Congress, etc.

Sec 102. (a) United States policy toward the African National Congress, the Pan African Congress, and their affiliates shall be designed to bring about a suspension of violence that will lead to the start of negotiations designed to bring about a nonracial and genuine democracy in South Africa.

(b) The United States shall work toward this goal by encouraging the African National Congress and the Pan African Congress, and their affiliates, to—

(1) suspend terrorist activities so that negotiations with the Government of South Africa and other groups representing black South Africans will be possible;

(2) make known their commitment to a free and democratic post-apartheid South Africa—

(3) agree to enter into negotiations with the South African Government and other groups representing black South Africans for the peaceful solution of the problems of South Africa—

(4) reexamine their ties to the South African Communist Party.

(c) The United States will encourage the actions set forth in subsection (b) through political and diplomatic measures. The United States will adjust its actions toward the Government of South Africa not only to reflect progress or lack of progress made by the Government of South Africa in meeting the goal set forth in subsection 101(a) but also to reflect progress or lack of progress made by the ANC and other organizations in meeting the goal set forth in subsection (a) of this section.

Policy Toward the Victims of Apartheid

Sec 103. (a) The United States policy toward the victims of apartheid is to use economic, political, diplomatic, and other effective means to achieve the removal of the root cause of their victimization, which is the apartheid system. In anticipation of the removal of the system of apartheid and as a further means of challenging that system, it is the policy of the United States to assist these victims of apartheid as individuals and through organizations to overcome the handicaps imposed on them by the system of apartheid and to help prepare them for their rightful roles as full participants in the political, social, economic, and intellectual life of their country in the post-apartheid South Africa envisioned by this Act.

(b) The United States will work toward the purposes of subsection (a) by—

(1) providing assistance to South African victims of apartheid without discrimination by race, color, sex, religious belief, or political orientation, to take advantage of educational opportunities in South Africa and in the United States to prepare for leadership positions in a post-apartheid South Africa;

(2) assisting victims of apartheid;

(3) aiding individuals or groups in South Africa whose goals are to aid victims of apartheid or foster nonviolent legal or political challenges to the apartheid laws;

(4) furnishing direct financial assistance to those whose nonviolent activities had led to their arrest or detention by the South African authorities and (B) to the families of those killed by terrorist acts such as "necklacings";

(5) intervening at the highest political levels in South Africa to express the strong desire of the United States to see the development in South Africa of a nonracial democratic society;

(6) supporting the rights of the victims of apartheid through political, economic, or other sanctions in the event the Government of South Africa fails to make progress toward the removal of the apartheid laws and the establishment of such democracy; and

(7) supporting the rights of all Africans to be free of terrorist attacks by setting a time limit after which the United States will pursue diplomatic and political measures against those promoting terrorism and against those countries harboring such groups so as to achieve the objectives of this Act.

1. According to the document, United States asked South Africa to do all of the following **except**

    A. end military action against neighboring states.
    B. give all people the right to form political parties.
    C. uphold apartheid laws in some areas.
    D. release black trade union leaders.

2. According to the document, what does the United States promise to do to South Africans who were arrested by authorities for nonviolent activities?

    A. free them immediately
    B. give them financial assistance
    C. retrain them for new occupations
    D. reunite them with their families

3. The United States would like the African National Congress to reexamine their ties to the

    A. South African Community Party.
    B. Pan African Congress.
    C. African National Congress.
    D. Government of South Africa.

4. What would the United States most likely do to individual aiding victims of apartheid?

    A. negotiate with the individual
    B. deport the individual
    C. arrest the individual
    D. assist the individual

5. Which section authorizes economic sanctions against South Africa?

    A. 101
    B. 102
    C. 103
    D. none of the above

6. Summarize the United States views on apartheid. Use details in the document to support your answer.

_____

_____

_____

_____

_____

_____

_____

_____

_____

_____

_____